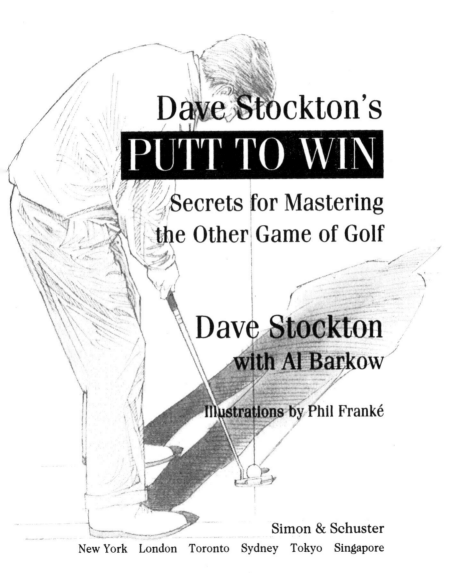

Dave Stockton's
PUTT TO WIN
Secrets for Mastering the Other Game of Golf

Dave Stockton
with Al Barkow

Illustrations by Phil Franké

Simon & Schuster
New York   London   Toronto   Sydney   Tokyo   Singapore

SIMON & SCHUSTER
Rockefeller Center
1230 Avenue of the Americas
New York, NY 10020

SIMON & SCHUSTER and design are trademarks of Macmillan Library Research
USA, Inc. under license by Simon & Schuster, the publisher of this work.

Designed by Levavi & Levavi
Manufactured in the United States of America

10 9 8 7 6 5 4 3 2 1

Library of Congress Cataloging-In-Publication Data

Stockton, Dave.
Dave Stockton's putt to win:
secrets for mastering the other game of golf/
Dave Stockton with Al Barkow.
p. cm.
1.   Putting (Golf) I. Barkow, Al. II. Title.
GV979.P8S86   1996
796.352'35—dc20   95-51167
CIP
ISBN 0-7432-4528-8

For information regarding the special discounts for bulk purchases, please contact Simon &
Schuster Special Sales at 1-800-456-6798 or business@simonandschuster.com

Contents

Foreword

You're probably reading this book because you want to learn my putting mechanics. If so, you will not be disappointed. There will be many ideas about technique. Some probably will be new to you, but you should have no trouble making them part of your game, because my points about reading greens, gripping the putter, stroking the ball, and such are not complicated. And because the mechanics I describe here have contributed a great deal to my success as a player, I'm sure they'll help you, too.

But this book has not nearly as much to do with mechanics as it does with *attitude.* Many thoughtful players and golf teachers have said that golf is 80 percent mental and 20 percent mechanical. I subscribe to that equation completely, and with even greater passion when it comes to putting.

Ask yourself: Do you look forward to putting? Do you feel excitement in the anticipation of stroking a ball on the right line over a banked piece of terrain at just the right speed? That's the mind-set I believe you should have and the one I want to instill with this book, because the real fun of golf lies in fulfilling what you had in mind. The mechanics I teach will help you make more putts, and the more success you have, the better you will feel about putting.

There has been no clearer proof that this attitude works than my own experience in winning one of the most important championships in golf. Although I had already won one PGA Championship and nine regular PGA Tour events, as well as a number of amateur competitions, most of them largely the results of good putting, the putt I had to make at the Congressional Country Club in 1976 to win my second PGA Championship was the culmination of all I had worked on up to then. Allow me to recall that moment.

When I won the PGA at Southern Hills in Tulsa, Oklahoma, in 1970, it was a totally different situation. I started the final round with a four-stroke lead, built that to seven by the turn, and still led by three strokes with one hole to play. At Congressional, I had to par the last hole to beat Raymond Floyd and Don January, who had completed their play. The first order of business for me on the eighteenth hole, a long par four that Congressional members play as a par five, was to hit the fairway. I had hit only one on the back nine that day, so I decided to play safe and chose my 3-wood. Having opted for accuracy over distance, however, meant I was left with a longer approach shot. I had 230 yards to the pin, with a lake guarding the left side of the green. I also was worried that, by trying to keep from hitting the shot to the left, I would push the ball to the right, so I decided not to hit a wood for my second shot, but instead lay up and trust my pitching and putting. I hit a long iron to about 15 yards short of the green, leaving me a 25-yard pitch to the hole. The greens were perfect, and my mental thought for the pitch was to keep the ball below the hole. I did, although I left a little longer putt than I'd intended—around 13 or 14 feet.

The putt I faced to win the PGA Championship was almost dead straight, maybe a hair inside the right edge. As my playing partners putted out, I lined up on my own putt because I don't like to lose my rhythm when I get into contention. Since I was going to putt last, I wanted to be ready when my time came. I still recall how after I'd hit the pitch shot, a lot of the gallery had left to get in position for the first playoff hole. But when I'd finished reading my putt I told my caddie, Mike Rose, that they were wasting their time. My ball was going dead into the hole.

I was very calm when I took my stance. I went through my regular routine, took one look at the hole, then sent the ball on its way. As I looked up, with the ball about five feet from the cup, I knew it was in. I felt a special thrill I had never felt before, knowing I was going to win a major title no one thought I would. As the putt fell, I turned to face the people across the lake and raised my arms in victory. I had fulfilled what I had in mind. It was the greatest satisfaction I had ever felt in competitive golf.

I was born and raised in San Bernardino, California. My dad was the golf professional at Arrowhead Country Club, two doors down from our house. Groundskeepers from the golf course would mow our backyard on their way to some of the holes. You could see the ninth and first greens and the tee of a par-three hole from the back of our house. That's where I cut my golfing teeth.

When I was four or five years old, I had only two clubs, a driver and a putter, and I would play out to the first hole then back to the ninth—hit a drive, tee it up in the fairway and hit another one and so on, then putt. I don't remember using any other clubs, although I must have had access to anything I wanted. I also don't remember if Arrowhead had a practice range. I guess it did, but I didn't use it much. I do remember there was a putting green, and I spent hours on it. Even at six and seven years old I would challenge anyone who came along to putt against me. I enjoyed that more than anything and always would hold my own. I'm sure that's one reason why I became such a good putter.

My father, Gail, was a powerful influence on me. By the time I was in my teens, he had gotten into the retail sporting goods business (as a golf pro he couldn't play golf when he wanted to), and I worked in his store during the summer when I was thirteen. The next summer he informed me I would be working for our next-door neighbor, Duncan Gibson, who owned a lumber company, and that became my summer employment every year until I was a senior in college. I played hardly any golf during those summers, and the kids who I could beat in June when school let out could cream me when school began again in September. It made me mad, but there was nothing I could do about it.

When I was fifteen something happened that probably cemented making golf my career. We were on vacation in San Clemente, and one day at the beach, while in about two feet of water, I was hit in the back by someone's surfboard and knocked senseless. At the time, I didn't really know how badly I'd been hurt, but I felt a lot of pain afterward, and a little more than a year after the incident I finally had my back X-rayed. Basically, it was broken. My six lower left side ribs had been broken or cracked, and by the time I had the X-ray, cartilage had formed around the bones. The doctors decided not to operate, and to this day, my left leg is an inch shorter than my right leg. (I didn't realize this until 1967, when I was out on the pro tour. I was suffering from back problems and went to an orthopedic surgeon. Since then I've worn a lift in my left shoe, and the back problems have been reduced to almost nothing.)

I was adequately long off the tee before the surfboard accident, but soon, because I was less flexible, everyone started to pass me. I was a good putter before the injury, but now I had to focus even more on that part of my game. I also stopped playing baseball and basketball and concentrated entirely on golf. My father still wouldn't let me play more than three tournaments a year, but not because of my back problems. I wasn't happy at the time, but now I understand what my dad was up to. He was not allowing me to get overgolfed and lose my desire to play. When I did get the chance, I played with a vengeance.

There were two summers when he made an exception to his rule, more or less. After I graduated from Pacific High School, in 1959, I was allowed to play in the Arrowhead junior championship, which I won. I also got to enter the Hearst national junior tournament and won the local qualifying medal at Riviera with a 75 after taking a 10 on the first hole. In the match-play segment, I won every match by the fifteenth hole. That earned me a trip to Albany, New York, for the nationals. I'd been to Mexico and

Arizona to fish and hunt but never had been farther from home than that, and now I was getting to fly across the country, all expenses paid. Fantastic!

In the first round I shot 80 or 81, I think, and was twenty-fifth in a field of twenty-six. But three rounds later I was in second place. I won a huge trophy and a trip to New York City to appear on *The Ed Sullivan Show*. My mother ended up upset at me, though, because I bypassed the Statue of Liberty and went fishing with a friend in New Jersey. My mother had wanted me to see all the sights.

That was a great summer. My dad also let me play in the National Junior, at Stanford. I was seventeen. I remember beating a fellow named George Boutell, who at the time was a fifteen-year-old hotshot, and finally losing in the fourth round. I had a good tournament and felt that, with a little practice, I might become even better than I thought I was.

The other summer my dad let me loose to play was in 1963, when I was in my junior year at the University of Southern California, where I had gotten a scholarship. I played a couple of tournaments in California and in the U.S. Amateur, for which I qualified along with Roger Cleveland, a fraternity brother who would become a very successful golf-club designer and manufacturer. We drove all the way to Des Moines, Iowa, for the championship in his Volkswagen Beetle. In the first round, Roger drew a bye and I drew William Hyndman III. I'll never forget it. In the program it said, "David K.

Stockton, San Bernardino, Calif., times qualified, once." That was it. Hyndman's listing ran six or seven lines. He had won everything, state titles, the North-South, whatever. But I was determined not to lose after driving all that way, and I beat him 4 and 3, shooting five or six under par. Eventually, I missed an invitation to the Masters by one match. I lost on the twenty-first hole of my fifth-round match to a plumber from Cleveland named Walter Stahl.

It was after that tournament that I first thought I could make a living playing golf. But my dad, following the same train of thought that made me work all those summers—he wanted me to realize that life wasn't going to be handed to me, and that I would have to learn the value of a dollar—was adamant that I finish school and become an attorney. He and my mother grew up in the Depression and didn't see much of a future in golf. But I was just as adamant about trying the pro tour, so we compromised. I would try the tour but I would return to get my degree. It took an extra semester, but I graduated with a law degree in February 1964.

My father was an excellent golfer and a gifted golf instructor—and the only teacher I've had. I have pictures of him with Walter Hagen when they played an exhibition together. I won the Arrowhead club championship once; my dad won it nine times. My lowest score at Arrowhead was a 64. Dad shot 63 four times. He won the Pac-10 conference championship when he was at USC, and then I won it; we were the first father and son tandem to win that title. Dad was also an all-American while at USC, as I was, and when my oldest son, David Bradley Stockton, Jr., also made the all-American team, we became the only father, son, and grandson to do that at USC in the same sport. I take a lot of pride in that.

In thinking years later about what my dad taught me about the mental game, I realized how brilliant a teacher he was—although I didn't think so at the time. Case in point: I remember vividly his telling me that my grip was too weak with my left hand and that I should strengthen it. How long do you think that takes for a fifteen-year-old? Five minutes. So pretty soon after he told me about the grip change, I went up to him and said, "I got it. Now what do you want me to work on?"

"Nothing," he said. "Go out and have some fun."

"What do you mean?" I asked. He asked to see how I had my hands on the club, I showed him, and he said it was perfect, go play. I'm living in the same house with him, and for the next three weeks he wouldn't tell me anything else. Then, all of a sudden he said, "Okay, let's have another look at your swing." And if there was something he thought needed changing, he'd tell me. If not, he wouldn't say a word. I thought at the time that I had a pitiful parent who didn't want to tell me all he knew. I wanted it all at once, but of course he was way ahead of his time. He was professing what the sports psychologists would be telling everybody twenty-five years later, that it takes twenty-one days to change a habit.

When I was growing up at Arrowhead, I would play with a group of guys who were from one to three years older than me. I was the shortest hitter in the group, but I had them mentally. I had more of an inner drive, part of which came from my father having me focus on the fact that golf wasn't a physical game, but that it was like playing chess with yourself. He would tell me not to get mad because everybody was outdriving me. He said the pressure I could put on them with my next shots—especially if I could stick an approach close to the hole—offset my lack of length off the tee, because none of them could putt as well as I could. Consequently, I developed a philosophy whereby I said that with my short game I could whip an opponent every time. So I would never give up mentally.

I also came to realize that putting was the thing you most remember when you finish a hole. It is far more important to go to the next hole after making a good approach shot and/or a good putt for a birdie or an up-and-down par than it is to have hit the longest drive on the hole. I go by the same philosophy to this day.

I feel bad that my father wasn't alive when I got to work with Mac O'Grady, who has helped me a lot with my game. I would have loved for them to discuss things. Mac uses a thousand words where my dad would use five. Mac has positions he wants you to learn. My dad would tell five different people different things. "Don't let your knee move" to one guy, "Tighten your two left fingers" to another guy, and so on, but they both knew—or, in Mac's case, know—what they were talking about.

When I first went out on the pro tour I was hitting only about eight greens in regulation a round, but I was scoring well and picking up checks, and people would say to me, "Man, you're lucky to have such an unbelievable short game." I'd say, "Thank you very much, that's good to hear," which is not the response most golfers would make to such an evaluation. Most golfers don't like to hear about their short games being good. They want to be congratulated for being able to hit the big drive or an 8-iron 170 yards. Being told you are a good putter seems to imply that if you couldn't putt you wouldn't be any good at all.

I understand those who extol hitting. I know it is a very gratifying physical and psychological experience to really stripe a drive. I've hit a few of those myself. But if you want to be a complete golfer, you have to master every part of the game. Frankly, I think hitting a perfect putt dead on line with good speed that takes a three-foot break—just as you figured it would—and dives into the hole is a pretty thrilling thing. You do, too, if you're really honest with yourself. After all, when was the last time you jumped in the air after hitting a long drive?

I just love it when I play a big hitter who outdrives me by 40 yards but who I beat because I get up and down after missing greens and make a good share of birdie putts on the greens I do hit. They say it isn't fair. I say that putting is as much a part of golf as hitting the ball hard and long. (In fact, it's more; almost half the strokes played in an average round of golf are with the putter.) To me, it doesn't make any sense that if you need to hit two shots to reach a green, it should take the same number of shots to get the ball in the hole. On the basis of pure physical effort—coordination, flexibility, strength—putting is a piece of cake. Hitting the ball long and accurately is a lot harder and should take more effort. But golf has nothing to do with manliness. It has to do with making the lowest score possible.

People tend to forget that scoring is the name of the game. Maybe it's because of the great emphasis that is constantly put on driving distance in the sale of clubs and balls and in the reporting of golf. Telecasters will go on at great length about how far someone has hit his drive or the fact a player can hit a short iron a remarkably long way, but you seldom hear much chat about how well a guy reads a green or how fine his touch is.

I realized early on that someone who wasn't a good chipper and putter would have to be unbelievably good at the long game to succeed. It so happened that I was a good iron player and could knock a lot of shots stiff to the pin, but I still *wanted* to be a good putter. Why? Because that would take a lot of pressure off my long game.

You may ask if working on my long game would achieve just as much, because it would take pressure off my short game. In theory, that's true. But in practice, I believe you can become a better all-around golfer by working on your putting. It's the *easier* way to go.

The biggest contribution I can give you is the idea that if you are mentally up to being a better putter, then you will be. Mechanics will help bring this about, of course, and I will point out some basics of technique and a few ideas that are a bit different, but it all really begins with *wanting* to be a good putter.

CHAPTER 1

The Power of
Positive Thinking

Good putting starts with *seeing* the ball going into the hole before you take your stance—in fact, before you even take your putter in hand. When you reach the green and see where your ball is in relation to the hole (and have erased all thoughts of the shot that got you there), you are already starting to putt. You begin to read the terrain over which the ball will roll, judge the line the ball should take, and get a sense of the speed it will roll. Then you conjure up a mental picture of the ball following the terrain, rolling at a certain speed, and falling into the cup as if it has already happened. What you see at this point is the *entire* putt, not any particular portion of it. I will talk later about breaking down putts into thirds as a way of reading a green's undulations and the speed of the surface, but they are part of the details that make up the overall vision of the putt.

An apt metaphor might be a long bridge that you are about to drive across. Say it's the George Washington Bridge over the Hudson River or the Golden Gate Bridge over San Francisco Bay. You already know how to get to the entrance, what lanes you must use when you're on it, and how fast you must drive, so at this point you don't look at the bridge's parts—the pylons and cables, the driving lanes, the guard rails. You don't see the entrance ramp except in the most cursory way. If you begin thinking about all those details, you're liable to get distracted and risk having an accident. It's like the story of the centipede who was asked how he walked with all those legs going at once. He got confused and began to stumble. Basically, all you see is the bridge itself, in its entirety, a beautiful sweeping span, and the far end, where you will conclude the journey. That is ultimately how you should look at every putt once you've made the preparations to play it. The path between your ball and the hole is a bridge taking you from the entrance to the exit. Except the exit in this case is the entrance—the hole.

Then you let it happen. When you get into position to stroke the ball, there should be no thoughts at all regarding the mechanics of putting—grip, stance, length of stroke, etc. You are now in the realm of intuition and feel. This is not an idealistic

When preparing to hit a putt, you want to see it not as a series of details but as a whole. The overview can be likened to approaching a bridge you are about to cross. You don't look at the pylons and cables, the guard rails, or the driving lanes. You see the entire bridge, from beginning to end, with special focus on the exit (or, in this case, the entrance) at the far side.

concept, some sort of otherworldly notion. Researchers into athletic performance have found that if you have a clear image of what you want to accomplish—a 12-foot left-to-right breaking putt falling into the left side of the cup, say—you will produce the physical mechanics necessary to realize that mental picture. You may not get the end result every time, but having a clear image of what you want to happen before acting increases your odds for success considerably. Good putting therefore is the result of mind *before* matter. This belief is at the core of how I putt and how I teach putting. It is not for potential or low-handicap golfers only.

There is a situation in golf that I like to use to "prove" my point. You have a shot of 75 yards from a good lie in the middle of the fairway to a big, wide-open green. The cup is cut in the center of the putting surface. It is a simple shot, but you hit the ball poorly and come up short of the green or maybe wide of it in a bunker or on the green but too far from the hole considering the length of the shot. The next time around you have the same shot to the same green, but someone has planted a 12-foot-high pine tree that is 20 yards ahead and directly in your line. Now you begin to calculate the shot very carefully. You ask yourself how the tree is going to affect your approach and what you have to do to get your ball clear of it. You decide to go over the tree rather than around it and create a mental picture of the trajectory the ball will have. You choose the club for the shot, set up at the ball, and strike it solidly, purposefully. It never touches the tree and ends up close to the hole. You have a putt for a birdie.

The lesson? With the tree in your line you were forced to think hard about it and find a way to avoid it. Finding that way included creating an image of how the ball would fly. You then went through the process of fulfilling that image—choosing the club and producing the swing mechanics to get the job done. When there was no tree in your way, there appeared to be no need to envision the flight of the ball, where to land it, where it should stop. You took the shot for granted.

That's why trouble shots are sometimes easier to pull off than simple ones—you are forced to see your best option. You put mind before matter. The message here applies even more to putting, because you never will have such an obvious hurdle in your way as a tall tree. So you must train yourself to see the putt in your mind before hitting it.

There is an interesting and perplexing phenomenon in golf. Golfers who improve their full-swing shotmaking often get worse at their putting or never get better than mediocre. Why? There are a couple of reasons. One is that when a golfer is not hitting the ball well from tee to green he doesn't hit many greens in regulation. He may become a good chipper, because he does it so often. However, he makes the mistake of thinking he's a good putter when in truth he is not; it is the good chipping that is keeping his score down. The second reason is that when the golfer works on his full swing he starts hitting more greens in regulation. He is now putting for more birdies, but usually from 25 or 30 feet. No one makes a lot of those. So the golfer starts thinking he's a poor putter—even though he's scoring well. As soon as he thinks that, that is exactly what he becomes.

I speak from my experience. I remember playing in the Tucson Open during my first year on the PGA Tour in 1964 and calling my dad one evening and telling him how frustrated I was because I had hit 16 greens in regulation and shot 73. He asked me how many putts I had under 10 feet on the greens that I hit in regulation. I couldn't recall any. His point was that it wasn't my putting that was at fault, that just hitting greens as big as those in Tucson is not enough to put yourself in birdie range. (However, if I'd hit sixteen greens on a course with small greens and *still* had shot 73, then there might have been cause for concern.)

Another strange aspect about putting involves how we compare making par from off the green to two-putting for a par. From a touchy lie, you make a good chip or short pitch that finishes a foot or two from the hole. You save par and are very pleased with yourself; you made a good recovery to avoid a bogey. But when you miss a 15-foot birdie putt then tap in for an easy par, you walk off the green only vaguely dissatisfied. Your reaction should be stronger. Although you have done what the score-card calls for, you should be disappointed that you didn't make that putt for birdie.

Paul Runyan, who had one of the best short games in golf history, said that every putt from 12 feet or less should be considered "makeable" and anything outside that is in the two-putt range. He also said that the chances of holing from 13 feet are the same as from 30 feet or 50 feet. Mr. Runyan was a student of the art of putting and undoubtedly based his judgment on a lot of personal experience and observation of others. But I would say, first of all, that because the greens are generally so much better nowadays that "makeable" to him would now be in the 15- to 20-foot range. To me, however, all putts are makeable.

I believe you should—must—think you can make every putt you look at *no matter the distance.* If you keep that in mind you will end up making more of them from lengths you would in the past have thought to be out of range. This is not merely "blue sky" wishful thinking.

I can hear you saying "Sure, Stockton, it's easy for you to say. You've made a lot of putts over a long period of time and have thereby developed a positive attitude." Well, it's true that success has a way of breeding more success. At the same time, I have missed my share of short putts, and I will miss a few more down the road. But after every miss, on the very next putt, on the very next green I see the putt before I hit it—and see myself making it. And I often do.

Is that all there is to it? Make a lot of putts and gain the confidence that produces even more holed putts? Not exactly. There are real, earthbound ways to produce good results, although, as you will see, they are not necessarily scientific.

For instance, a few years ago I shot a first-round 73 in the Los Angeles Open, at Riviera, with 36 putts. I was mortified. That evening I went back to where I was staying, at the home of Ron Rhoads, an old friend and an outstanding teaching pro, and Ron and my wife, Kathy, convinced me that I should study the Sybervision video I had made on my putting. The Sybervision technique avoids dialogues; only the stroke itself is seen, from a variety of angles and distances. The idea is that the viewer, just by watching the stroke, will subliminally ingest the mechanics, form, and tempo he or she sees over and over again. (Older pros, from the Jackie Burke, Jr., generation, called such learning "monkey see, monkey do.") Anyway, I was not especially in the mood and resisted, but we eventually did run the video. I turned on some of my favorite music, leafed through a magazine, had conversations with people in the room, and periodically glanced at myself putting on the video. The next day, I shot 67 *with twenty-four putts*. I hit only eleven greens, so my ballstriking was not as good as it had been the day before, but my putting (and my chipping) improved significantly, and the score proved it. If anything, the story shows how feel for putting is not a conscious effort, which produces tension, but more often is the result of an indirect, in a way offhand, approach.

A similar incident occurred while I was playing in the 1995 Ameritech Senior Open, in Chicago. In the first round I shot 73 with three birdies, one eagle, and *four three-putt greens.* I was upset and that evening called Dr. Deborah Graham, a psychologist with a special interest in golf with whom I have been working for a few years. She said only this: "Tomorrow, *don't try* to make any putts. Just put a good roll on the ball." That was it, basically. On Saturday and Sunday I made a total of fifteen birdies and had *no three-putts.* By not trying! In truth, it's hard to do this, and there is a fine line between not trying and being nonchalant, but I would say that, given the option of trying hard or not trying at all, the not trying end of the spectrum will be more effective.

Those are two specific ways I was able to deal with previous failures. But generally speaking, I also try to grasp the realities that go along with putting. We all know we're not going to be one hundred percent successful in everything we do, golf or otherwise. We are human and make mistakes. We must accept that. There are a lot of sad stories from the pro tours of players who came out with excellent swings and fine games, started well with a lot of high finishes or maybe a win or two, but decided they wanted to be *perfect*. It's an impossible dream they thought could be fulfilled, so they started making significant changes to their technique. At first it was a struggle, which was expected. But rather than going back to doing things that got them out there in the first place ("Dance with who brings you," as the saying goes), they continued to seek perfection. In the end, they lost their stuff altogether and were off the tour. Ben Hogan once said that even in his best rounds of golf he hit perhaps three or four shots exactly as he'd wanted. He would have liked to have hit every shot perfectly, but he knew it wasn't going to happen. He lived with that understanding and did pretty well.

There are some things in putting that can never be explained. It has been shown many times, for example, that when you roll ten balls down a Stimpmeter, the chute used to measure the speed of greens, at exactly the same speed and angle and over the same distance and swatch of grass, some will roll into the cup and some will not. I'm sure you've hit the same putt twice on a practice green and are convinced that the stroke for each was exactly the same. Yet one went in and one didn't. Why?

Most of us like to find some "scientific" reason for everything that happens. Maybe on the putt that didn't go in, the face of your putter hit the edge of a dimple on the ball and sent it just enough off line to miss. Or maybe the ball ran over a bit of uneven grass or a depression so slight you couldn't see it, and that took it off line just the hair it missed by. But why didn't the depression or uneven grass affect the other ball, the one that holed? Maybe the putt that went in was hit just a tad faster and was able to overcome the defect in the surface. Maybe one ball weighs a gram more than the other, which would affect the speed at which it rolls. I can go on with even more possible "scientific" and unscientific reasons for one putt going in the hole and the other staying out, but the fact is, you never will figure it out.

How then should you respond to the inexplicable vagaries of putting? You must have a streak of fatalism in you, a willingness to accept what happens as something you can't completely control. That's hard to do. Golf is a game that begs for control, of your swing, of the flight of the ball, of your emotions. Some people are by their nature more demanding of their lives than others and want as much control as possible. Others are of a mind to accept that things don't always work out as planned, and just go ahead and keep trying. Clearly, it is the latter personality or attitude that has the best chance of making good in golf. Or at least enjoying it more. Life is full of disappointments, and all things considered, a missed putt here or there is one of the lesser ones.

But you must at the same time be willing and able to assess the degree and nature of your misses. If you are satisfied that you stroked a putt as well as you could and it misses, you must ask yourself if you read the putt properly and accept that perhaps you didn't. Very often golfers will blame a poor stroke for a missed putt, when in fact they simply started it on the wrong line. Or maybe you had the right line but hit the ball a bit too hard and putted through the break. If you came up an inch or so short on a putt of some length or left a shorter putt below the hole, then you may not have followed through completely or didn't keep the putter low through the stroke or slowed your stroke, decelerated, at impact or simply misjudged the speed of the green.

Any of these things may have happened, but in the end *you must never blame yourself.* I can't tell you how many top tournament golfers over the years found "alibis" for missed putts or poor shots. Some have told their alibis to the press and have been castigated as arrogant and above blame. But the criticism is mostly unwarranted, because these alibis are part of a mind game that athletes play with themselves. Some are conscious of doing it, others do it instinctively, but in any case they are working on the premise that you don't want to break down your self-esteem by always taking the blame for your errors. They may know that on a perfect green they missed a relatively easy putt simply because they hit it poorly. They will assess the mistake and acknowledge to themselves that they must work on the mechanics or the mental slip that caused it, but at the same time they find an excuse that lets them off the hook, so to speak, and project that to the forefront of their psyche.

By the same token, when they have success—hit a fine shot, hole a tough putt—they give themselves credit. A lot of credit. This, of course, is meant to bolster self-esteem.

Another way to develop a positive attitude about your putting is to put faith in the system you are using. There are certain putting mechanics that I think are better than others, but you're always going to be making adjustments. And I encourage that. I don't follow my own fundamentals to the letter every time I stroke a ball, so why should I expect you to? Mechanics vary from day to day simply because we don't always feel the same; our adrenaline flow and metabolism rate vary; some days our hands feel fatter than on other days. It does little good to force an address position or a stroke pattern onto a body that simply does not want to do it that way. Room must be left for physical and psychological divergence in our makeup and for intuition and instincts of the moment to play a role in performance. That implies *trusting* your instincts and intuition.

Odd though it may sound in a world that is becoming increasingly more "programmed," I have found that trusting instinct and intuition is more reliable than a robotic adherence to a fixed,

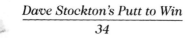
immutable set of physical mechanics. The best golf is played by people with imagination; who have a willingness to improvise, to fit their action to the moment at hand and how they *feel* at that moment. Mechanics are an intrinsic element in putting, but more important than the specific details of those mechanics is that you can repeat them without thinking about them. The idea is to filter those mechanics into your subconscious so that when you are on the golf course trying to make a good score, you are free to imagine the shots you need. Poor players hit and hope and think that only when they become better ball strikers and/or putters can they begin to picture successful shots. But that's not the way it works. You have to picture good shots before you can start hitting them. Imagine the putt going into the hole, and I guarantee you'll see it happen more often.

CHAPTER 2

Reading Greens

There Is More Than One Center of the Hole

There is no more important component in support of the concept of *seeing* the ball going in the hole than reading greens.

In fact seeing, or "imaging," a putt before you hit it by reading the terrain over which the ball will travel determines the mechanics and the quality of the stroke itself. Your confidence level is high whenever you are sure you have the right line for a putt, and you miss many putts because you are not sure of the break. So let's talk about reading greens before we get into mechanics.

There is no scientific way to determine precisely

how much a putt will break or where the ball will begin to break. But the more you work on trying to obtain all the information that is available, the better a "guesstimate" you will make. There are ways to come very close to the correct read.

I begin with the premise that just about every putt has some break to it. The only time I aim at the center of a hole on a putt I think is straight is when the putt measures three feet or shorter. If you aim for the center of the hole, only half of it is available to you if you push or pull the ball. In fact, I always hope there is some break, and if I'm not sure, I just play for some. On short putts with only a slight break, I simply aim to keep the ball somewhere inside the hole on the side where I think it will break.

This brings me a point that cannot be stressed enough in putting—and something I don't think many people consider or even realize. That is, your ultimate target, where the ball will actually enter the hole, is *not necessarily its conventional or diametric center.* By that I mean, most golfers think of the center of the hole as if they are playing on perfectly flat terrain; the point to shoot for is on the circumference that is nearest to the ball (we'll call this the "conventional" center). But that doesn't take into account the contour of the ground. Now if a putt has break, *the center of the cup is where the ball will enter* if the break is played properly. Thus, on a left-to-right breaking putt the left edge is in fact

On a breaking putt, your ultimate target is not the diametric center of the hole but rather the point where the ball is expected to enter. This is not only a reality, it provides you with a psychological boost—you know you have more hole to use to sink your putt.

the center of the cup. But don't think that you have to squeeze the ball into a corner of the hole; this would not only distort your read of the putt but present a psychological problem, too. Instead, gain confidence in knowing that you have the entire hole at your disposal on a breaking putt, if you roll the ball on the correct line at the right speed. (Some readers may take the term "center of the hole" literally, to mean the empty space in the middle of the hole itself. However, it is more commonly understood by golfers that the term in fact means a point at the edge of the hole.)

Golfers who hit the ball at the proper speed but who aim for the conventional center of the hole on a breaking putt almost invariably miss on the low side. If the ball does go in, it has been hit too hard and has rolled, as we say, "through the break." That's good for that particular putt, and you may be heartened by the success, but in the long run, hitting the ball through the break is going to produce more failures than successes. Some of those fast-rolling charges will hit an edge of a hole and, more often than not, spin out. And the more you ram the ball rather than roll it, the faster the tempo of your stroke gets, and you begin to lose both touch and accuracy. If you keep in mind that on breaking putts the center of the hole is at the point where the ball will enter after navigating the break, you will instinctively understand that you must roll the ball to circle around and come into the hole's true front door.

All the above is predicated on playing enough break, and in my experience most golfers underread and underplay the break. Why? For one thing, most golfers are more line conscious than speed conscious. That sounds paradoxical. If they concentrate so much on the line of a putt, why don't they get their breaking putts high enough? If they roll the ball too slowly, the ball breaks too much and if they roll it too fast, which is more common, it doesn't break enough. By never getting the speed right, they never get an understanding of the line. On the other hand, if they concentrated on and improved their speed, they would begin to recognize and understand the correct line.

Another reason golfers do not play enough break is because they do not have consistent mechanics. There is a tendency to let the blade of the putter follow the contour of the terrain on which the putt is being made. For instance, when putting on a slope where the ball is below your feet—a left-to-right putt—the putterhead is swung back to the outside, or away from your body, and toward the ball on the same curving path. At impact the blade is not going onto the correct line of the putt; instead, it is going under, or to the right, of the hole. The opposite applies on right-to-left putts; the blade goes back to the inside of the line, then moves to the inside at impact and beyond. The ball goes left of the correct line. In each case, the putt may have been read correctly but the stroke didn't conform to the read —it was corrupted by the stroke path.

Reading the Speed

In gauging the speed of a putt, there are some genuine things to look for and feel, such as the grain of the grass and slope of the putt and the firmness of the putting surface. But there is also a *sense* of the speed and that is more or less impressionistic; it is how it *feels* to you. This is impossible to quantify, but it is a sense that feeds off more tangible stuff. Let's deal with that.

Contour obviously affects the speed of a putt; an uphill putt will have to be hit more firmly than a downhill putt. The degree of slope will give you a sense of how fast or slow the putt will be.

Grain affects speed too, although for the most part this is an issue only with Bermuda grass. The grain on Bermuda tends not to run in a consistent direction, and different strains of Bermuda have different amounts of grain. In any case, however, the direction of the grain affects the speed of a putt. If you're putting with the grain (the grass blades pointing in the same direction as your putt), the speed will be faster than if you're putting into the grain (the blades pointing toward your ball). If you're putting across the grain, the ball will break in the direction the blades are pointing. When reading grain, consider also the speed at which the ball will roll. You can putt through the grain, just as you can putt through the break, and if you don't hit your putt firmly enough, the grain can "throw" it off line.

An awkward putt is one over sloping terrain where the grain runs down the slope, as it normally does. It will be a little faster once it begins to take the break, especially when the ball turns toward the cup. This is a tricky putt you should practice; it's one of the reasons the best players try to leave their approach shots "below" the hole.

The best way to see which way the grain is running on Bermuda greens is to look closely at the grass. On bent grass greens, the grass appears "shiny" when the grain is running away from you. You can get another read from the hole itself, especially in the afternoon after a lot of rounds have been played. If one edge of the hole is razor sharp and the opposite edge is beaten down—jagged and rough—the beaten down edge is the low side of the hole and where most of the balls that day have made contact when, one hopes, they enter the hole. It is the side toward which the grain is running.

Two final points on grain. One, the most crucial area to read is near the hole. This is where your ball should be slowing down and is therefore most susceptible to the effects of grain. Second, although agronomists have developed strains of Bermuda almost as consistent as bent grass, even these surfaces have grain and are a little slower.

The *firmness* of a green is another way to read speed, but this is strictly a matter of feel. On some greens, you can feel the speed just by walking on them. Oakmont is like that—you're kind of glad you're wearing spikes, so you don't slip and fall. In fact, you can get the feel of a green's speed by how your spikes go into the ground. Is there a certain resistance? Does it feel brittle? Then the green likely will be fast. If you feel you're walking on a cushion, if the green is moist, the green likely will be relatively slow.

There are other ways to read speed. A good way is to check the location of greenside bunkers. Those that butt up against the putting surface, or jut into it, usually create a ridge on the green at that point, which will influence speed more than other undulations, because these ridges are firmer and faster than others.

You might also use the experience of the practice putting green, *providing it is consistent with the greens on the course.* If you haven't played the course, ask the club pro if the practice green has the same speed as the real greens.

You also can draw on your experience from the holes you already have played. But keep in mind that different greens on the same course can have different speeds (although ideally they shouldn't), depending on the contour and grain. What's more, if play is moving slowly, keep in mind that grass grows during the day and the greens on the back nine, when you finally get there, are probably going to be a little slower.

Many golfers judge green speed by watching their playing partners' putts. I don't think this is a good idea (and that holds for reading the break, too). You can't really know whether the other golfers in your group have hit their putts solidly or not, and of course you can't possibly know their feel for a green and how they react to it. Neither do you know if the type of ball they are using reacts differently from yours. If they're putting with a hard, two-piece ball and you're playing a three-piece balata, there is a significant difference. In any case, the information you get from watching others is uncertain and can cloud your own judgment and sense of feel. Always go with your own insights.

That said, here are some other ways to read a green.

Reading the Sun and the Geography

You should begin reading a green before you ever step foot on it. Indeed, you can begin to read all of them on a course in a general way before you even get to the first tee. If you are going to be playing on Bermuda grass greens, which usually have a lot of grain, you want to know which way is west. The tips of Bermuda grass grow toward the setting sun, and by mid-afternoon they will be heading west.

Grain also runs towards water. At the Riviera Country Club, in Los Angeles, for example, the greens become much easier to read once you realize that the course is built in a canyon that runs to the Pacific Ocean. You may not be able to see the sea from the course, but you should know in what direction it is and that everything breaks toward it. If you are on the right side of the eighteenth green, for instance, and putting toward the water, it may appear you have a flat run to the hole. But I can guarantee you that the putt will be faster than a similar one on a course built on a Kansas prairie.

If you're playing a course at the base of a mountain range, putts are going to break away from the mountains. The Broadmoor, in Colorado, is a good example of this. The architect may try to counteract this and build slopes in his greens that turn directly into the mountains. He may succeed to some extent in changing the course of nature, and a putt may well break toward the mountain, but not nearly as much as the slope would make it appear. The mountain is always going to have its way to some extent.

In some cases architects have defied nature completely. On the courses at PGA West, in Palm Springs, Jack Nicklaus, Arnold Palmer, and Pete Dye were working with basically pancake-flat terrain, although it does drop off gradually toward the nearby town of Indio and the Salton Sea. If they'd let nature take its course, all putts would break toward Indio and the Salton Sea, as is the case on most courses in the area. But Nicklaus et al. built so many large mounds into their greens that the Indio–Salton Sea "read" does not apply. In such cases, you find the break in them by looking for where the water drains off—the lowest point on the green. As a general rule, on all greens that are designed correctly, or at least in the classic mode (the back higher than the front), the water will drain toward the front. That is the "master break." Any putt that goes across the width of the green, from one side to the other, probably will break toward the front of the green.

That should give you a broad overview of reading greens. Inevitably, you are going to have to be more precise in getting your read of greens. With the "master break," for example, there will almost always be other contours that affect putting. Golf architects like to make things more interesting by "enhancing" what nature has given them to work with. But that is what makes golf so interesting—no two courses or holes or greens are exactly alike. In any event, now I want to discuss locations from which to read a green when you are down to the nitty-gritty of determining the line.

Always Read from the *Low* Side of the Slope

Like everyone else, I read every putt from behind the ball, looking to the hole—down the line of putt. I also get a read from one side of the putt—*always the low side;* never the high side. Therefore, if the putt is definitely breaking from right to left, I look at the slope from the left side. Looking from the high side can be very confusing. An analogy: If you stand on the lip of a canyon that slopes down and away from you, you can't see very much of what is below you. What you do see is distorted; it is difficult to judge distance. But if you look at the upslope on the other side of the canyon, it's a panoramic view and you see everything in good perspective and in detail. You can get a good idea of how big the trees and rocks are, and how far they are from you. Another analogy: If you read a book that is angled with its bottom away from you, you can't read it very well. Angle the top away from you and it's an easy read. The same thing applies to putting. Look at the line of a putt from the high side and you don't see as much break as there actually is. You will see a lot more from the low side.

Looking at a putt from the low side tells you whether you are putting uphill or downhill, a slant that will also give you input on the speed of the putt. You will also get another picture of the curve of the terrain in respect to how much it breaks left-to-right or right-to-left. I'm not sure why this is so; on the surface, it doesn't seem a way to get that read, but you do. In fact, very often you will get a better picture of the putt's curve from the *low side* rather than from behind the ball.

A lot of golfers look at a putt from four angles— from down the line, from behind the hole, and from both sides. That's at least one view, and perhaps

On all putts with any amount of break, besides the conventional read of the line from behind the ball, you want to get a view from the side—and that must always be the low side. *This gives you a better overall perspective of the path you are going to putt the ball on and of the degree of slope.*

two views, too many. For some reason, a putt that from down the line looks like it has a right-to-left break, appears to break in the opposite direction when you look at it from behind the hole. Many golfers have reported this phenomenon.

Nevertheless, in certain situations I do read the line from the hole back to the ball, and especially when I have a downhill putt. Here my "canyon" theory applies. In looking up the hill, I may see a bit of break to one side or another that I wouldn't see looking downhill from behind the ball. Also, if a green has a lot of moguls or I'm just not sure of the break, I will look from the opposite end. But for the most part, I get my read from behind the ball and from the low side of the slope. It reduces confusion to have only two views.

A caddie can help you read a putt when you're not quite sure of the line. And if your caddie agrees with your read, you go into the putt with much more confidence. But you must be careful. You have to be sure you are both on the same wavelength, see things the same way, and speak the same language. What's more, the caddie has to have a sense of how you roll the ball so he can judge how much break to play. I put a softer roll on a putt than a lot of players and have to play more break than those who hit putts more firmly.

Plumb Bobbing. This has become a popular way to read the line of a putt—although I'm not sure all golfers do it correctly. Plumb bobbing gives you a general read of the terrain—whether it breaks one way or another—but it's not a precise method.

You must first ascertain if you are right- or left-eye dominant. The simplest way to do this is to hold your index finger up vertically in front of you and, with your right eye closed, align your finger with an object—the flagstick, say—with your left eye. Now, open your right eye and close your left eye. If your finger appears to have moved to the left (and you see the entire object), you are left-eye dominant. If your finger remains in place, you are right-eye dominant. Conversely, if you begin with the right eye open and aligned on the flagstick (or whatever) and your left eye closed, if it appears that your finger has moved to the right when you open up the left eye and close the right, again you are left-eye dominant. If the finger remains in place, you are right-eye dominant.

To plumb bob, hold the putter at the tip of the handle and let it hang vertically in front of you with the shaft bisecting the center of the ball and the hole. Align the putter in relation to the ball and hole using only your dominant eye; the other eye closed. If you are right-eye dominant, as I am, you will see only the left half of the ball. Now, look up the shaft to where the hole is "covered." If you see all or a large portion of the hole, you have a right-to-left putt. If you see very little or none of the hole, the putt breaks left-to-right. If you see half of the hole, the putt is dead straight.

Break Putts into Thirds

I like to break down putts into thirds. A 30-footer, for example, is made up of three 10-foot segments. Each segment gets its own read. Your main consideration with the first third of the putt is the speed of the surface; the break is not very consequential, because the ball is moving at its fastest and contour will not have much effect on it. Contour is more important on the second third, because the ball is beginning to slow down. But the last third is where it really counts most. I give about 85 to 90 percent of my attention to the last third of a putt and particularly the last two or three feet. At this point, very near the hole, the ball is coming to a stop—or should be—and is highly susceptible to the contour of the green.

A lot of golfers who use the thirds method do so on longer putts, but I think it is worth doing it on every putt of 10 feet or longer.

Getting a Read in Adverse and Unusual Conditions

On hard, fast greens, speed is crucial to success. Putts are not going to break as much as it appears, no matter how softly you roll the ball, because the ball is going to have some pace to it. To counter this I apply some stroke technique. I try to keep the putter very low to the ground during the stroke, even letting it ride on the grass a touch going back. I won't forward press quite as much as normal, if at all, because I don't want to take a chance on popping the ball, having it jump off the face. When a downhiller is really slick, I won't forward press at all, using the loft of my putter to produce a softer roll. I may even begin the stroke with my hands slightly back of center so that the loft of the putter kind of deadens the impact.

Wind doesn't affect the roll of a ball very much, except perhaps if you're playing in one of those West Texas "breezes." When a particularly strong wind is blowing with or into your line of putt, the ball will speed up or slow down a little. But mainly, the wind affects putting by moving your body during the stroke. If the wind is blowing from heel to toe, at your back, you're better off than when it's from toe to heel, or into you, but in both instances the solution is to widen your stance a little. And don't forget to maintain your normal tempo. Just as in playing full-swing shots, golfers tend to rush their putting strokes when the wind is blowing.

Reading the Dew Line

If you're alert you can find some unusual ways to get a read on a putt. At the Phoenix Open one year, I was in one of the first groups of the day. The greens still had a little dew on them, and I was about to putt on one of them when I noticed a faint mark made by a ball putted earlier on the same line. It had missed by about four inches to the left, so I backed off and ended up playing about eight inches of break where originally I'd planned on playing only four inches! I knocked the ball in the hole.

In fact, a great way to get that sense of the real curve of a putt is to practice on dewy greens. You'll be surprised by how you underestimate the amount of break. It is a good lesson in learning to read greens.

Speed Reading

Putting begins with a feel for speed, for the pace of the ball as it rolls toward the hole. You often hear golf television commentators talking about a putt being a "speed putt," meaning that if it is stroked too hard it will not take the break or if hit too softly it will break too much. Either way, if the speed is not right, the putt is missed. They are correct, but they tend to limit speed putts to fairly short ones with a lot of break. To me, *every putt is a speed putt!*

Were speed and direction to be rated on a scale of one to ten, the speed (or distance, as they really are one and the same) gets a nine. Direction gets a one. Most golfers would reverse that equation, because they are so frantic to make the putt, they think finding the exact line is the answer. That would seem to make sense, but unless your read of the terrain is totally wrong, you're going to be pretty close to the correct line. Remember, the hole is 4.25 inches in diameter and the ball is 1.68 inches in diameter. So there is a margin for error of around 2.5 inches *if you have played the ball high enough and have it rolling at the correct speed.* What determines whether you stay on the line, but even more important, whether the ball has a chance of going in if it is on line, is how fast it is rolling. A putt that hits the back of the hole may fall, but it was moving at the wrong speed. It was *hit,* not stroked, and you should count yourself lucky that you got away with one.

There is a school of thought that says on short putts with some break you want to hit the ball firmly so the break is effectively taken out of play. That is simply poor thinking. As I've already noted, the golfer banging the ball straight on (and effectively putting through the break) is sharply reducing his margin for error. If he isn't dead center on line, the ball will in most cases not fall. He is not using enough of the hole. For a putt of one or two feet, I may sometimes put a bit more pace on the ball, but from three feet and more I want a soft roll.

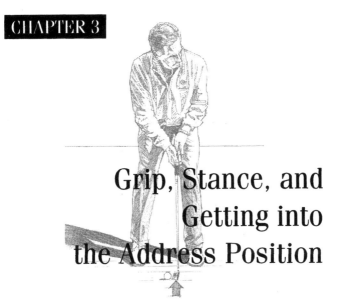

CHAPTER 3

Grip, Stance, and Getting into the Address Position

The Grip—It's in the Fingers

Producing a soft roll means having a good feel for speed. That thing called feel is extremely difficult to describe, and equally hard to teach. Almost by definition, feel is not quantifiable. It's like being in love with someone. You can't say exactly why, and you're probably better off not trying. Still, while I am convinced the best golf is played by feel, the game also has an engineering nexus; even I think in terms of parts of the body and the club moving in certain interconnected ways. So the best, and possibly the only, way to acquire a good feel for putting is, in an engineering sense, through your hands.

They are your only connection with the club that is going to propel the ball. That being the case, how you hold the club is crucial to how much feel you have.

This is why the putter should be held in the *fingers* of each hand, and with as many fingers as possible. The fingers are the most sensitive part of your body when putting. They give you the best sense of the weight of the clubhead and where it travels during the stroke.

As I will point out in more detail later, I believe in cocking the wrists slightly in the backswing. I am not a wristy putter by the conventional definition of that term, but I am definitely not a shoulder putter. Shoulder putting is very much in vogue these days. Its advocates claim that putting should not be a small muscle and nerve action, that the hands should be taken out of play. Well, lots of luck to them. To me, this is too mechanical. In trying to numb their hands, shoulder putters cut off the only contact they have with the club. Part of their technique involves holding the club in the palm of the left hand. I don't think this is a very secure position, no matter what type of stroke you use—the putter is liable to jiggle. But more important, you don't have sufficient feel for the clubhead through a thick palm.

No, I believe you should use the small muscles in putting. The handle of the putter, therefore, should run on a slight angle across the callus line of the last three fingers of your left hand, crossing the lowest pad of the forefinger. The club is held entirely in the lower part of the fingers of the right hand. Each thumb is positioned down the center of the handle and flush to it. This is why I recommend a putter grip with a flat front, a paddle grip, rather than a completely round one. The thumbs fit better.

When both hands are in their final positions, they form a unit. The back of the left hand is flat and facing the target, the back of the right hand is facing directly away from the target. In a sense, the hands are mirror images of each other. Your grip will be unbalanced if, for example, the right hand is in the neutral position as described above but the left hand is turned to the left so much that its back is more or less facing the ground rather than out toward the target (or, the palm is facing up rather than away from the target), in the so-called weak position. Or vice versa. When the hands are not balanced, they will not work as a cohesive unit; they will "fight" each other during the stroke. However, it's okay to turn the left hand under into the "weak" position if the right matches it and is "strong": that is, it is turned to the right so much that its back faces the ground (or the palm faces up) to the same degree as the left hand. Corey Pavin uses this type of grip. It may look awkward, but it's balanced.

I prefer the neutral grip because it is so uncomplicated and reduces the margin for error. The

To use the small muscles effectively in putting, the club should be held as much in the fingers as possible. In the left hand, the putter should run on a slight angle across the callus line of the last three fingers, ending on the lowest pad of the forefinger.

All *the fingers of the right hand, especially the lower part of the fingers, are on the handle of the club. Maximum feel is acquired this way, so that full control of the hand in the stroke itself is possible.*

The completed grip: Each hand is at the same angle in relation to each other and to the target; the back of the left hand is flat and facing the target, the back of the right hand is flat and facing directly away from the target. The hands are in balance, or neutral.

Also, each thumb is positioned straight down the center of the handle. The paddle-type grip with a flat front facilitates this important positioning of the thumbs.

An example of an unbalanced grip: The right hand is in the neutral position, its back facing directly away from the target. However, the left hand is turned well to the left— "under" the handle in a "strong" position and not in balance with the right. In this position, the hands cannot work as a cohesive unit.

Pavin-type grip is two negatives that make a positive. The neutral grip on the other hand is two positives making a superpositive hold on the putter.

Making the Connection

Most golfers keep their fingers very close together on the grip. I like to spread them slightly, just as they would be when you throw a ball underhanded. Spreading your fingers allows your hands to cover more of the handle and gives you more control of the club, enhancing the feel. In a way, I'm more interested in controlling the grip end of the putter than I am the clubhead. When I have hit the ball and continue the stroke past that point, I want the grip of the club (and my hands) to remain vertical. With most golfers, the butt end of the putter (and their hands) are pointing back toward their belly button in the follow-through. That indicates they are flipping the clubhead at the ball and raising the putter up. Anything you can do to keep the putter going low through impact is good, and a slight spreading of the fingers on the handle is one way to promote this.

Your hands, however, should be closely joined. I recommend a reverse overlap—the forefinger of the left hand atop the little finger of the right. (It's called a reverse overlap because it is just the opposite of how you hold the club for full-swing shots if you

The reverse overlap grip: The connection of the two hands is made by overlapping the forefinger of the left hand directly atop the little finger of the right hand, not in the crease between the forefinger and middle finger. Note that the left hand is completely on the handle—there is no overlap of the butt end; and there is a slight spreading of the fingers of the right hand to cover more of the handle and provide as much clubhead feel as possible.

use an overlapping, or Vardon, grip.) Why not use the same overlap you use for full-swing shots? Because the Vardon overlap allows the right hand to be active in the swing, and that gives you power and distance. Putting, however, is not about power and distance. It is about precision. And the reverse overlap grip makes the left hand more dominant, while subsuming the right hand as much as possible.

When the right hand dominates the putting stroke the left hand (or wrist) breaks down as the ball is struck. The head of the putter comes up instead of staying low to the ground through impact. The result is poor direction and distance. You often see this type of stroke among golfers with the yips. When I teach, I sometimes have students put their right hands in their pockets and putt solely with their left hands. They almost invariably putt better.

Quite a few golfers like to expand their reverse overlap by running the left forefinger across three fingers of the right hand. Others will overlap both the forefinger and middle finger of the left hand; Tom Weiskopf does this. In both cases, the thinking is sound: Make the left hand as dominant as possible. But I don't recommend those overlaps, because you lose feel. With the overlap of two fingers you have only eight fingers (counting the thumbs) touching the club—the five fingers on the right hand, three on the left. And one finger overlapping two or three fingers creates tension because the fingers are stretching more. In putting, tension must be avoided at all costs.

Using the *Whole* Club

This may seem like a small thing, but I believe it is important that your entire left hand holds the club. The entire heel pad should be on the handle, with none of it overriding the butt of the club. I'm not sure why so many golfers do this. A lot of baseball power hitters have the heel of their lower hand riding over the knob of the bat, to get more wrist action in their swing. That is exactly what you do *not* want in putting. You want complete control of the club. It's the left hand that works the stroke, furnishing the direction of the stroke and controlling its flow. The right hand provides stability, but basically it just goes along for the ride.

In fact, it's not a bad idea to choke down a little on the handle *without bending any lower from the waist.* Choking down extends your arms a bit more, gets them a little straighter, and makes it easier for the left hand to go through in the stroke. If your left arm is bent too much at address, you may cup the left wrist and allow the right hand to be dominant. How far should you choke down? You don't want to get too far down or you'll lose your posture. Some golfers putt well from a deep crouch, but I don't believe you can see the line as well as when you stand relatively tall at the ball.

Grip Pressure

Grip pressure is crucial to good feel. It especially affects distance but is also a factor in making or missing short putts. In short, there should be no feeling of pressure or tension when you hold the club. The putter must be held only as tightly as you would hold a small bird: firmly enough so it can't fly away but not so hard that you will hurt it. Someone should be able to pull the putter out of your hand fairly easily; that's how lightly it should be held.

You may think that such a light grip restricts control, that the putter might jiggle around in your hands. But it doesn't happen, because when you make the stroke you instinctively firm up your grip. The same thing happens when making a full swing. If you begin with a tight hold, the increased pressure will become so great that you instinctively loosen up to get relief, and then the club might come loose in your hands.

A lot of golfers hold their putters too tightly because they're worried about missing the putt. Usually they're not good putters in the first place and are frustrated. It's a mental problem but becomes much less of one as your putting improves. The more putts, especially clutch putts, you make, the less anxiety you will feel.

But there are other reasons for holding the club too tightly. A common one is because a putterhead is too heavy. A lot of golfers use heavy-headed putters, perhaps because they play on slow greens. Or they think this will encourage making a smooth stroke and still get the ball to the hole. Whatever the reason for using such a putter, it must be held firmly to control it, and that creates tension. I use a relatively light putter, because I want the feeling that I am swinging the putter rather than it swinging me. I use a slightly heavier putter on slower, Bermuda-grass greens, *but I put lead tape under the grip to counterbalance the head weight and maintain a feeling of lightness.*

Putting on very fast greens is another source of tension that results in a tight grip. Golfers worry that they'll hit the ball too hard, so they tighten the grip to better control the pace of the stroke. But tightness means loss of feel, and the result often is the opposite of what the grip pressure was meant to create. If you also use a heavy-headed putter on fast greens, this problem is magnified.

The size of the grip on your putter could also create a too-tight hold, particularly if the grip is too thin. However, with an overly fat grip you can't get your hands comfortably around it and that too will cause you to grip it tightly. We'll discuss how to determine the width or circumference of the grip for your putter in chapter 5.

One more thing on grip tension. The right hand should be lighter on the handle than the left, although both should be relatively soft. A good way to be sure your grip is soft is to "milk" the handle as you stand over the ball and are about ready to stroke it. Relax and tighten your hands, *without changing your hand positions.* You will feel the difference between light and tight and find the degree of pressure that is right for you. Everyone has his own sense of what is too tight. On the whole, though, you want to strive for a sense of lightness.

The Stance—Be a Rock

The stance has one purpose: to prevent moving during the stroke. This is absolutely vital to putting well as movement is the bane of bad putters. The trouble is, you don't always feel that you're moving.

People move when they putt because, for one thing, it is inherent in all sports that involve swinging a stick to hit a ball. The trouble with golf is that, on full-swing shots, you move considerably. The habit of such movement then carries over to putting, even though now you want to stand absolutely still. On a full-swing shot your right knee goes forward in the downswing and the left knee kind of backs up to get out of the way. I've noticed that in putting, many golfers make a similar movement with their left knee. Not nearly as much, but enough to pull the head of the putter in toward the body at impact. The left knee must remain absolutely still throughout the stroke.

Head movement is another serious problem. Even a little movement can hurt your stroke and your chances of success. More often than not it is the result of the golfer being anxious to see the result of his stroke and looking up *before* impact. You must wait until the ball is well on its way before looking at it. Easy to say, but not as easy to do.

A conventional method for keeping the head still is to force yourself to listen for the ball going in the cup. But many golfers still follow the putterhead going back with their eyes and continue watching it as they bring it to impact. That is movement, too. Not only must your head remain still, so must your eyes. There is no real mechanical way to cure this; only willpower will keep your head and eyes still until the ball leaves the clubface.

Of course, there is some movement involved in putting. The arms and hands should move, and on extremely long putts there will be a slight shoulder swing and perhaps a little leg movement (which is the result of narrowing your stance for putts of this length).

Your stance also is crucial to remaining still. First of all, 60 percent of your weight should be on your lead side—the left side for right-handers.

And the weight should be on the balls of your feet rather than on the heels. You should almost feel that you are on your toes. I know it sounds as though you will be tilting forward and unstable, but that feeling of instability prompts you to stand still. Your instincts tell you that you don't want to fall down, so you make sure you don't.

If I can see a golfer's front spikes when he addresses the ball I am looking at someone who is not a good putter. His weight is on his heels, which promotes a stroke in which the putter is pulled inside the line going back and to the left after impact, instead of moving straight out with the blade square to the target.

Ride a Horse

A way to enhance proper weight distribution is to bow your legs slightly at address. The feeling is that of sitting on a horse. I bow my legs such that the outer rim of each of my shoes is on its edge.

Standing slightly bowlegged will go a long way toward preventing the left leg from straightening during the stroke. It provides a dead-solid foundation from which to make a stroke without moving your body.

Eyes Over the Ball

Putting your weight on the balls of your feet also help get your eyes directly over the ball at address. This is key to seeing your line correctly and strok-

A good, solid stance serves one vital purpose: to prevent moving during the stroke. The slightest motion during the stroke will cause the putt to roll off line. Note that the putter head is on the opposite side of the ball. As we will see later, this position is an important part of the setup process.

ing the ball on that line. Here's a drill I use for this. Address your ball, then drop another ball from underneath your dominant eye. The ball should land *on* the ball you are about to putt. For most golfers, the ball that is dropped will land about three or four inches inside the ball already on the ground; this means they're looking at a line three or four inches inside the line they want to putt on. Looking at the correct line from the wrong angle is a major cause of missed short putts.

Open at Address . . . But Just a Bit

In putting you don't aim with your feet as you do, in part, with the full swing. You aim with your eyes and the clubface. Thus, I like to open my stance slightly, pulling my left foot an inch or so back from the target line. This allows you a better look at your line and the target, and your body doesn't get in the way of the stroke. But don't take too open a stance, for then you'll feel like you're hitting out into a void with your hands and arms. By keeping your shoulders, hips, and knees square to the target line, you'll be able to keep your left hand guiding the club, and your squared knees will provide the sight line to trace your stroke along your line of putt.

Some golfers use a closed stance when putting, the right foot pulled back from the target line. This aims your body to the right of your target and also makes you hit "against" yourself. Your body gets in the way of your stroke, and you abort it just after impact with the ball. But you really want the putter to move all the way through the ball, staying low through impact.

Knee Flex

At address your knees should be evenly flexed. Standing straight-legged, or with very little flex, allows you to see your line clearly, but it tends to encourage leg movement during the stroke. On the other hand, flexing too much will result in poor posture. Try to find a happy medium. Taller players usually have to flex more than golfers of average height (unless they are using a very long putter) and they have to be careful not to bend too much at address. The bend for everyone should be at the waist, with the back as straight as possible. Making sure your eyes are directly over the ball will go a long way toward determining the correct degree of bend. Just be sure you don't slump your shoulders, which tends to crimp your arms.

Distance from the Ball

Most golfers stand too far from the ball when they putt. (The eye test described on the previous page reflects that.) The result is that your hands end up too low at address, and the lower your hands, the more the right hand dominates the stroke.

What is the correct distance to stand from the ball? Here again, getting your eyes directly over the ball will tell you. If you've bent too far forward, simply move closer to the ball. You'll know you're too close to the ball if you find yourself more or less looking back at the ball with your chin tucked in toward your chest. Not many golfers stand too close to the ball.

Width of Stance and Where to Play the Ball

There is no single standard as to how far apart your feet should be. Some days my stance is narrower than usual, because it feels better that way. As a general rule, though, the stance should be reasonably wide—the heels 10 to 14 inches apart for shorter putts. Many golfers widen their stances for very short putts in an effort to avoid movement, but you must be careful not to exaggerate this. If your stance is too wide, the lower body posture makes it harder to see your line.

I will narrow my stance for longer putts, to around four to six inches apart at the heels, so I can stand taller and make the longer stroke that usually is required. Standing tall also allows you to see the line better, which is important because there is more line to see. I'm not as concerned about moving here. A lot of other safeguards are still in place, such as the legs being slightly bowed.

Where should the ball be positioned? I think it *should always be inside your left foot* and as far back as the middle of your stance; it depends on how you feel and the nature of the putt. If you err at all, it is better to have your ball closer to the center, because you want to catch it early in your stroke to help you keep the clubhead low and moving along the line.

Golfers who play the ball well forward in their stance, off the left toe, generally make a very long backstroke and a short follow-through, if any at all. Because the backstroke is so long, the inclination is to decelerate in the forward stroke. This results in a kind of "pop" stroke. But when you pop, you also stop. You more or less recoil the club. Imagine throwing a dart and drawing your throwing hand back immediately after the release. Or imagine a baseball pitcher backing up *behind* the rubber after delivering a pitch. The best dart throwers and baseball pitchers keep their throwing hand moving toward the target, moving their bodies forward after release, allowing the momentum that has built up to continue. You don't have body momentum in putting, but the momentum of the clubhead must continue. If you hit at the ball, you stop the flow, and you'll almost always "flip" your hands and wrists at impact. Another analogy can be drawn from shooting basketball free throws. The good shooter doesn't stop the forward motion of his hands and arms after he releases the ball. His shooting hand continues forward after he releases the ball. The same thing must happen in putting, and that's hard to do with the ball too far forward in your stance.

One reason I don't want to be absolutely specific about ball placement is because the width of your stance plays a part. If your stance is very narrow, such as Ray Floyd's, you can't really position the ball four inches inside your left heel; it would be off your right foot! No, you just have to find the position that works for you, while making sure that the ball isn't too far forward.

What I will be specific about is this: Once you have settled on ball position, do not change it, whether the putt is uphill or downhill or breaks sharply. Contacting the ball at the same point in the stroke makes for greater consistency, since you won't have to make any compensations or adjustments. On extreme uphill or downhill putts simply take a longer or shorter stroke.

Get Your Hands Centered . . . and *Up*

When it comes to the position of your hands at address, *do not have them ahead of the ball* nor have the shaft at an angle in which the butt end is ahead of the ball. This is a very common address position and is essentially the position after the forward press is made. However, if you then forward press you will end up with negative loft on the clubface. I believe you *should* forward press, so at address you must have your hands and the shaft centered, that is, on a line with the middle of your chest or your belt buckle.

Also, your hands should be "high" at address; this is an important element in my technique. When I worked with Mark McCumber on his putting in 1994, the thing I had him work on most was getting his hands higher at address. He went on to win two tournaments and more than $1 million in the second half of that year.

Having your eyes directly over the ball and the sole of your putter flush to the ground helps get your hands up. But the key is having enough loft on your putter. If you have no loft, you will almost surely set your hands to the right of your chest. People do that instinctively. They want to see some of the clubface, just as they do when they play their woods and irons. But with the hands set to the right, the right hand becomes dominant. Being closer to vertical, say at a 75- to 80-degree angle to the ground, makes it easier and surer to keep your left hand from breaking down. At address, simply set your hands as vertically as you comfortably can. Golfers who tell me they miss a lot of putts to the left usually need to get their hands higher. The hands being close to vertical helps produce a pendulum-like stroke, and the putterhead stays low to the ground.

The Shoulders—As Level as Can Be

One last thing about what might be called the "static" part of the setup: *Your shoulders should feel level* at address. They can't be perfectly level, because the right hand is lower on the putter handle than the left, but too many golfers exaggerate the right shoulder drop, which in turn gets the left shoulder higher than it should be. They do this mainly because they believe they can see the line better. And they've seen Jack Nicklaus putt this way, and very well, for years. Be that as it may, I still think it's the wrong position.

The more level your shoulders are at address, the more level your stroke will be. To get the *feel* of this, sense that your left shoulder is heavy. It will drop down. Alternatively, just make sure you prevent your right shoulder from dropping down. It also helps if you keep your left arm close to your body at address and more weight on your left foot.

The idea is to keep from rising up during the stroke, which a high left shoulder encourages. With the right shoulder well down, the left shoulder is going to rock upward during the stroke—and then you'll never keep your putter low to the ground.

Why Cross-Handed Putting Works

Probably the best way to guarantee that your shoulders are level—and that the left hand dominates the stroke—is to putt cross-handed.

It's not a style I use, or plan to use, but I have no qualms about recommending it. All the other elements in my putting system can be performed with a cross-handed grip, everything from the bow-legged stance to the forward press to the "spot" putting I will soon discuss. Cross-handed putting has become very popular on the pro tours and for good reason. It brings excellent results.

Moving into the Setup— Keep Your Eyes on Your Goal

The idea of *seeing* the ball going into the hole before you even get into your address is also part of setting up to the ball. During almost all the setup moves *you should not take your eyes off the line of your putt.* You will glance at your ball during the setup, if only to make sure you don't accidentally bump it and incur a penalty. But your eyes and mind should be on the line of your putt and the hole. Don't worry. I promise that you will assume the proper alignment positions—if you have practiced them enough so they are intuitive.

Why stress keeping your eyes on your goal? One, you want to maintain your image of the ball rolling into the hole and falling over the front edge. Two, you want to avoid being too mechanical during your setup.

By looking at the line while moving into your address, you will instinctively know where to put your feet. Given you have a good grip, you will also instinctively align the face of the putter to the target. Once again, an analogy taken from basketball and the free throw. A good player never looks at where his feet are. As he handles the ball he never takes his eyes off the hoop. Michael Jordan has gone so far, at times, to prepare for free throws with his eyes closed. His mind is focused only on the hoop. The same mindset applies in golf.

This is not to say there are no specific details for moving into address. The most important is that you *always should walk to the ball from almost directly behind it,* while looking down your line of putt. This way you are able to keep the line in proper perspective. I don't understand how a golfer can approach his ball from a 90-degree angle to the line. You can't possibly get the proper view of the putt. What's more, this approach stimulates the impulse to concentrate on mechanics—where to place your feet, how far apart they should be, the angle of the clubface.

So, here is the procedure. Approach your ball from behind it, actually just slightly to the player's side of the ball. Keep your eyes on your target. At the ball, set your right foot at about where it will be when the address is complete. Your left foot is still close beside the right foot. As you set your right foot, place the clubhead in front of (or behind) the ball. The face will be aligned to your target. Then, *while looking at the hole,* place your left foot in position to the left of the ball. When your left foot is in position you are in your final setup. The left foot determines where you play the ball in your stance. For example, if you play the ball toward the center of your stance you will take a bigger step to the left with your left foot.

I have set down something of a formula, but it is not a strict one that must be followed to the letter each and every time. Where you place your left foot may be different, perhaps to accommodate a sloping terrain. You must trust your instincts in all such cases. You do not want to become too mechanical. You want to allow your intuition to guide you. From intuition comes the feel that is intrinsic to good putting.

Once your feet are positioned you may do some minor adjusting for ball placement, but basically you are set to go. While still looking at your line of putt and the hole, bring the putterhead from in front of the ball to behind it. Now you do look at your ball and take a quick survey of your various positions. Take one—and only one—more look at the line of putt. Then forward press and roll the ball.

Moving into the setup: Take a final read of the putt from directly behind the ball in a semi-crouch.

Keep your eyes not on the ball but on the line and the hole. Your left hand is on the handle in its basic grip position.

As you get to the ball, the right foot is set first. This is also where it will be when the stance is completed.

With the right foot in place, set the putter in front of the ball. Your eyes are still on the target. Then position your left foot.

Once again, because I don't insist that every little tic in my method of putting be followed, let me say that if you don't feel comfortable setting the putter down in front of the ball when you set up then don't do it. I do it because bringing the head back over the ball and behind it serves as a kind of waggle; it creates motion without changing any positions and puts some rhythm into the action. However, the last thing you want is the putter to be all but frozen on the ground before you begin the stroke. So, if you do like to keep the putterhead behind the ball all the time, I suggest you raise it slightly a few times to keep you loose and to prevent the blade from sticking on the ground.

No Practice Stroke Needed, Thank You

You have probably noticed that I have made no mention of a practice stroke. That's because *there doesn't have to be one.* Practice strokes take your mind off the line of your putt, your image of the ball going into the hole, your feel for the speed of the green. Even just one practice stroke puts your mind on the mechanics of the stroke, makes you conscious of stroke path, your grip, all the things that detract from your goal. Practice strokes also slow down the whole process of putting, which of course makes for tension. You never see a good pool

The final set-up position:
Your eyes are directly
over the ball, your
shoulders are as level as
possible. Feet are fairly
wide apart, and there is
a slight outward bow of
each leg. The knees are
slightly flexed. The ball
is played well inside the
left heel, and your left
foot is pulled back just a
hair from the target line
to produce a slightly
open stance. When the
clubhead is moved to
behind the ball, your
hands are close to
vertical and they and the
shaft are centered—they
are not forward or
ahead of the ball.

shooter taking practice strokes beside the cue ball, and neither should golfers do it when putting.

As we all know so well, Jack Nicklaus stands over his putts for what seems like an eternity. He can hardly be faulted, for he is one of the greatest putters the game has ever had. Nonetheless, I think it's better for most golfers not to emulate him. Jack is draining his mind of all thought before he begins his stroke. Which is fine, but if you are thinking only of your line and seeing the ball into the hole, you are already drained of all thought that can impinge on your stroke. To stand over the ball as long as Nicklaus does will give you time to think of all sorts of things that you *don't* want to think about. Now, if by your nature you are slow moving and need more time to get the stroke underway, go right ahead. But don't do it because Jack does. Golfers should go with the rhythm and routine they've practiced.

CHAPTER 4

The Stroke (and a Bonus Section on Chipping)

I never *hit* putts—I always *roll* them. There is a distinct and important difference. Golfers who hit their putts accelerate the clubhead in the impact zone. The clubhead travels faster than it did in the backstroke and even in the early stage of the forward stroke. Most of the time, if the ball misses the hole it goes well past it, leaving a three- or four-foot tester coming back. "Hitters" have stretches when they make most of their return putts, but over time the little ones wear them out. Then they get tentative with their first putts and *de*celerate the clubhead before impact. Putts begin to come up short. Confusion reigns. Arnold Palmer and Tom Watson are notable examples of the hitter syndrome.

Putting a good *roll* on the ball means that the speed at which the ball is moving always gives it a chance of going in. People often make that observation about my putting, and I love to hear it, because it is *exactly* what I am after. Whereas the hot-rolling *hit* putt must be on the perfect line and has to catch a lot of the hole to drop in, a putt that is rolling softly will always have a chance, even if a bit off line. It can work the edges of the cup. What's more, if a rolled putt misses it is unlikely to be far from the hole; the second putt should be a tap-in.

What is the key to rolling the ball? There are a few. There is the feel for the speed of the green and having confidence in your reading of the line. There also is an attitude of patience and the calmness of mind and body that stems from it. A putt is never a traumatic, do-or-die situation. You know that if you keep rolling the ball softly you will make your share of putts, and you can wait your turn (which will come more often than it will for the hitter).

On a purely technical basis, but one that derives from your feel and mindset, a soft roll is the product of the stroke having the same speed from backswing to impact to follow-through. On the longer putts you don't stroke faster and harder, *you just make a longer stroke.*

On all putts longer than three feet, you want to see the ball dying into the front of the hole on the intended line. On longer putts, stroke so that putts that miss never go more than 16 inches past the hole. With those two ideas in mind, you will stroke the ball with an even pace all the way.

The Backstroke—It Begins with a Forward Press

As I have already suggested, and will explain in more detail in the chapter on choosing a putter, I recommend you use a putter with at least four or five degrees of loft. The loft is not meant to get the ball "on top" of the grass quickly so it can begin rolling smoothly. (That was the purpose of loft in the days when greens were not as manicured as they are now.) I want loft because I believe the stroke should begin with a forward press—the hands and the club moving forward toward the hole before they begin to swing back. The loft on the putter reminds me to forward press, which does a few other things for the stroke, one of which is it helps make it more rhythmic. In musical terms, the forward press is the downbeat that gets an orchestra to play.

My stroke actually begins with a combination of the forward press and the application of a slight amount of pressure with the overlapping index finger on my left hand. I like to feel they both happen simultaneously, although if I were to break it down I believe the finger pressure sets the forward press

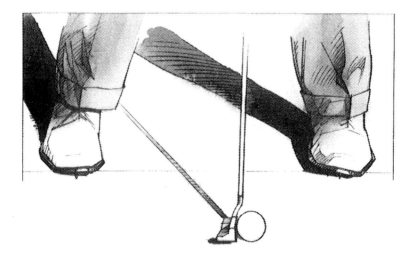

The forward press, in which the loft of the putter is reduced by some four degrees. The face of the putter, though, remains square to the target line, because the hands have moved laterally on that line.

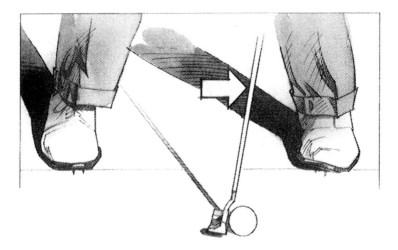

in motion. If that adds a certain complication you don't want to deal with, fine. Just think about making the forward press to begin the stroke. But make sure the forward press—imaginary or not—is part of your stroke.

How much should you press forward? You can tell by looking at your putter at address. If it has enough loft, you should be able to see most of the face. Now, press forward until the face disappears from view.

Have you delofted the putter? No, it is only *less* lofted. The correct forward press will take a putter with six degrees of loft, say, down to one or two degrees. It may even get to having no loft at all but it should not have negative loft. Negative loft will drive the ball into the ground, and it will bounce noticeably when it leaves the club. That is one clear indication that you have pressed too far forward.

There is no danger of opening or shutting the blade if the forward press is made directly toward the target line, but if your hands and the club move on an off-angle, the blade will either open or close. Here again, the loft will be the indicator. If you see only the right corner of the clubface, you have opened the blade. If you see only the left corner, you've closed it. Noticing that you have opened or shut the blade or have made too much of a forward press and drilled the ball into the ground probably won't help you on that particular putt. It is pretty difficult to stop the stroke once it has begun and to

The stroke effectively begins with the putterhead in front of the ball, and your eyes on the target.

The putter is then raised and placed behind the ball, which constitutes a waggle.

You then make a forward press—your hands move an inch or two laterally to the left, or toward the target— and almost simultaneously begin the backstroke.

start all over again. However, you will be prepared to correct the mistake with the very next putt you hit—if you are alert.

The Forward Press as the Waggle

One of the hardest aspects about golf, putting or otherwise, is that the action begins from a static situation. There is no moving ball to react to, as in baseball or tennis. However, within the framework of having to start from a standstill, there are certain moves that will help you produce a rhythmic flow to the stroke when it begins. The forward press serves that purpose very well. It is putting's equivalent to the waggle we are accustomed to making before hitting full-swing shots or to the pool player's sliding of the cue stick back and forth behind the cue ball before stroking it. In each case, tension is released and the takeaway is rhythmic. It follows that the rest of the swing will be the same. Poor pool players and golfers put their cue stick or club behind the ball and freeze it there. The result is a stiff, jerky takeaway and a swing that will be rhythmic only by happenstance.

Some golfers move their feet—raise their toes and drop them a few times as a way of getting into motion without changing their positions. It's not a bad idea, as long as it doesn't take too long. In fact, repeating whatever you devise as a "waggle" too often leads you to spending too much time over the ball. This in turn leads to thinking about mechanics, instead of seeing the ball into the hole.

All in all, I think the forward press is enough of a waggle. The beauty of it is that while it helps start the stroke with nice tempo, it also makes a vital contribution to the quality of other aspects of the stroke, in that it sets your left hand in a dominant position. Two birds are killed with the same stone, so to speak, and the overall action is less complicated. And having said that, I must emphasize that making a forward press and then stopping defeats the purpose: You essentially end up starting again from a standstill. Instead, *think of the forward press as the start of the backstroke.*

Backstroke Path: It's Not an Issue

This may sound peculiar, but I believe the backstroke is the least important part of putting *in terms of the stroke path.* You can take the blade back a little outside or inside the target line, as long as your forward stroke moves down the target line with the face square to the ball. I generally take the club back a touch to the outside then reroute it to the inside in the forward stroke. Ben Crenshaw and Billy Casper, among others, take it back a little to the inside, then reroute. That seems to be the natural tendency.

I like rerouting the stroke because it reflects a more intuitive, nonmechanical approach to putting. It is much better than trying to swing the club straight back from the ball and straight through. Many golfers try for this path, and there is a swarm of training devices designed to develop it. It is meant to get the ball rolling with perfect overspin. But I like to have a slight hook spin on the ball, not enough to take it off line, but enough to make it hug the ground—it doesn't bounce as much. In any case, a straight-back-straight-through stroke is something that has to be worked on; it is a conscious effort and, as such, is too machinelike.

Hooding It

In the backstroke, I recommend that you "hood" the blade a little. This is not to say the toe of the club is turned inward, or closed, so the face aims left of the target. Hooding here means the *entire* clubhead is tilted forward so the *entire* clubface is angled toward the ground. Or, the top line of the face tilts toward the target, while the bottom edge tilts away from it. Understand, this tilting is not as severe as it reads. But it is different from what most golfers, especially shoulder putters, try to do, which is to bring the clubhead (and clubface) back from the ball in the exact same position it was in at the address.

An even more distinctive difference is the

In the backstroke, the club is taken back with a slight cock of the wrists, a hinging that remains in place throughout the rest of the stroke. The face of the club is slightly hooded, the entire top edge more or less tilted forward, an event that basically occurs during the forward press. You don't consciously hood the blade.

"swinging gate" stroke used by Ben Crenshaw, Phil Mickelson, and Bob Charles. They "fan" the blade a little, slightly opening it so the face aims a hair to the right of their target. They then fan it back to square at impact. Such players as Crenshaw, Mickelson, and Charles can't be faulted for their stroke, but not many people have their marvelous control and tempo. By the same token, it takes a little more effort to keep the blade absolutely square from the start of the stroke all the way to impact. Hooding is safer for most golfers, and makes it easier to be consistent.

Wristy/Feely—Putting Is a Job for the Little Muscles

As I've said elsewhere, I do not describe myself as a wristy putter. I think of myself as a "wrist/feel" putter. I do cock my wrists slightly as the backstroke begins, which creates a small cupping of the right wrist and gives a nice flow to the backstroke. But, *I hold that wrist position through the remainder of the stroke.* That's the important thing. Truly wristy putters will cock their wrists in the backstroke and uncock them at impact. The putter comes up instead of staying low to the ground. The ball is usually hit rather than rolled. It is a very risky way to putt.

Shoulder putters do not want to use their wrists

or hands at all. As a result, they usually make a relatively long stroke on both sides of the ball. I think it is more difficult to adjust and refine this stroke for different situations—high-speed down-hillers, for instance. When I see someone putting with their hands, I am looking at a feel putter. Shoulder putters want to eliminate the use of the hands on the grounds that using them relies on the little muscles and nerves. They believe that is what causes the yips. I don't agree. I want my big muscles only to stay very quiet so all the feel in my hands and fingers propels the ball.

On the Yips

I never suffered from the yips, although shoulder putters argue that I am highly susceptible to them. The reason I don't get the yips is because I use a putter with a lot of loft, which prompts me to forward press. In other words, the yips are solely created by jumpy nerves, which can be exaggerated by "hitting" the ball instead of stroking it. Sometimes they are caused by poor mechanics, which are in turn the result of using the wrong kind of equipment. Simple as that.

The Forward Stroke—Low, Through, and to the Hole

Very early in my golfing life, my dad impressed on me the importance of keeping the putter low to the ground for the entire stroke and to do it by making the left hand dominant. In practice sessions he would hold the butt end of a club at the same height as, and a few inches from, the emblem of my glove. He would tell me to stroke the ball so the emblem on my glove would hit his club on the follow-through. If I hit the center of the emblem, I was right on. If I hit under it, I was raising up. In time, I got to keeping the club so low that I would hit Dad's club above the emblem on my glove, almost with my wrist. The idea was to get the left hand going toward the hole without varying the height of my hands from address position through to the finish of the forward stroke.

I have developed another drill for that purpose, in which I hit putts and put the clubhead on the ground after the ball has started rolling. I'll describe that and other putting drills in the chapter on practice.

Hit the Spot

Spot putting means something different to me than it does to most golfers. It is fairly common practice to pick a spot somewhere in the line of a putt, a

In the forward stroke, the head of the putter is kept low to the ground to and through impact, and the wrists definitely do not unhinge.

*Throughout the forward stroke, the back of the left
hand continues directly down the target line.*

dark piece of grass, say, maybe halfway to the hole
or within a couple of feet of it, and aim to roll the
ball over it. Do that and maybe the ball will go in the
hole. There is nothing wrong with that approach, I
suppose, but I think it detracts from seeing the ball
into the hole itself. I believe that on breaking putts
you should see the entire curve of the line all the
way to the hole.

Spot putting is something I do almost exclusively
on shorter putts, from 12 feet and closer. I can guarantee you that it is very effective, because it keeps
you from moving. It is not a drill, it is something
you do in play, on the golf course, although it is a
good idea to practice it as much as you can before
incorporating it in your game, as it does take some
getting used to. It is this: I pick a spot an inch or
two in front of my ball and on my line of putt, with
the intention of seeing the ball roll over that spot.
Furthermore, *I look at that spot and not at the ball
when I make the stroke.* That's right, I do not look
at the ball when I stroke it.

Remember when Johnny Miller made a point of
putting with his eyes closed in competition? He
tried it a few times and did pretty well. The idea
was that it presented him from being "ball-bound,"
staring so intensely at the ball for so long that your
body and mind freeze. Another method for avoiding
this is to look at the hole when you putt. I've seen
players try this and do very nicely. The point is, if
you are looking intently at the ball when you begin

When "spot putting," I keep my eyes focused on a spot an inch or two in front of the ball throughout the stroke. This keeps the stroke smooth and is very effective on putts from 12 feet or closer.

your stroke, your natural impulse is to *hit* it. When you are not looking at it, that very human urge is taken out of play. The stroke is very smooth, I can assure you, and you will hit the ball solidly and on target. And why not? You have your grip and stance in place, you know where you want the ball to go, the stroke itself takes no real exertion, and the backstroke is short enough that you won't miss the ball.

I am not saying you should never look at the ball when you stroke it. On long putts I do, but even then, like most people who are hitting balls with sticks, I don't always see it as a sharply outlined object exclusive of everything else. I look at it in a kind of passing way. I notice it and acknowledge its presence.

In any case, my spot putting technique is not meant to assure getting the ball on line, although it does. I don't expect to hit my spot precisely every time; if I miss it by a tad, it won't make a difference in the outcome of the putt if only because it is so close to the start of the roll. The main purpose is to make a smooth and complete stroke without any movement of my head and body. Nor do I spot putt all the time. If I start out a round putting really well, I won't spot putt because I prefer to avert anything that might give me a feeling of being mechanical. But if I miss one or two from in close, then I'll go to spot putting for a few holes to get back on track. It can be helpful on longer putts, but again, I tend not to spot putt from outside 12 feet. It is remarkably effective from short range.

I had been spot putting for some time when my son Ron suggested a refinement that has made it even more effective. (It even has helped my regular, non-spot putting.) Ron suggested that to better focus on the spot in front of the ball I should position my head a fraction more forward (to the left) at address. He had noticed that my head was sometimes getting a little behind the ball rather than right over it. That is a natural tendency, because everyone senses they will see the line more clearly by looking from behind it. But the more you do it, the more your body begins to tilt to the right. Then a lot of other body angles can go off. With my head a tad more forward and my eyes on the spot in front of the ball, I am in no danger of tilting backward; I stay in good posture, with more of my weight on the left side.

Length of Stroke

I am often asked if the length of the stroke correlates to the distance and speed of a putt. The answer is yes, though I tend to not think about the length of the stroke except on longer putts. If you are putting by feel and have *seen* the putt to the hole well before you stroke it and have incorporated into your system the idea of never going more than 16 inches past the hole, the length of the stroke will be appropriate. The more important thing is that the distance the club goes back is the same in the follow-through. There should be a balance to its overall length.

Obviously, I don't favor a short backstroke and a longer follow-through. Some players think the short backstroke guarantees they won't move, that it gives them a better chance of keeping the blade square to the target, or that it will assure that they accelerate the clubhead at impact and won't leave the putt short. Whatever the reasoning, that type of stroke breeds a quick punch or pop impact, which makes it very difficult to control speed and distance. The ball usually is hit too hard.

Nor do I recommend the long, loose backstroke of a Ben Crenshaw or Phil Mickelson, even if the follow-through is symmetrical. The danger here is deceleration of the club at impact. Those two players seldom have that problem, again because they have been putting that way all their lives and have a special touch. But the average golfer who plays once or twice a week in season will have a problem being consistent if he tries that style.

There are no specific numbers to put on stroke length, e.g., seven inches back, seven through for a particular distance. It is a matter of feel for distance (and speed) and your vision of the putt. Most people take the club back too far, mainly because they position the ball too far forward in their stance. The follow-through then tends to be too short.

You must be aware of stroke length, however,

when you begin to putt poorly. Once, my son David was not putting well and I had a look at his action. His backstroke was maybe six inches longer than his forward stroke. I put a tee in the practice green at the distances of each side of the stroke, to illustrate how much he was off. I then put a tee on each side of the ball at the same distance from it. He kept his stroke within those bounds and his putting improved immediately.

On Tempo

There is only one thing to say about tempo in the putting stroke: Move the putter at the same speed back and through. To recall a well-worn cliche, but one that is true, you swing the putter back and through as though there was no ball, and the ball that is there just happens to get in the way.

The tempo should be mellow. That is not a very scientific term, but here again I remind you that putting is very much a function of the mind, which responds very well if not better to nonscientific language than to engineering terminology. I try to picture everything I do about putting with a sense of calm. That's why I don't linger over the ball at address. It might appear that I am going quickly about my business, with no practice stroke, only one look at the hole, and so on, but appearances can be deceiving.

Evaluating Results and Making Adjustments

Ben Hogan, who often was referred to as the mechanical man for his *seemingly* machinelike approach to golf, said that golf is a game of constant adjustment. It certainly is. Everyone must have a basic framework for playing golf—a routine for getting into the address position, how to begin the swing, and so forth—but within that framework some room must be left for any necessary adjustments. They can become necessary after only one shot, although it usually takes a pattern of misses to develop a better understanding of the problem. However, that pattern can be just two shots of the same kind.

I constantly monitor how I'm missing shots and make notes—mental or otherwise. If I'm missing putts to the left, I will get my hands more vertical at address. That is almost always the solution. (I will say this, though. In general, if I miss a putt on the left side I am a fairly happy camper. My stroke was okay—I had to be stroking "out." I did not raise the club up, did not push it right or pull it inside to the left. I just didn't start the ball enough to the right, probably because my hands got a bit too low at address. Missing left is better than missing right, in other words.) If I'm missing to the right or if the ball is bouncing as it comes off the clubface, my forward press is probably too excessive or I'm opening the clubface by pressing off line. Or my hands may be too vertical. It almost always gets back to your fundamentals.

My dad taught me that the stronger you get physically from playing a lot of golf in one stretch or when you start feeling strong psychologically because you are playing well, the more you widen your stance. And the more you widen your stance, the tenser you become. Similarly, if you're not in great physical shape because you haven't played much lately (or have played too much), you are liable to lose your posture as a round progresses and crouch more at address because you're tired. It's like when you drive a car a long distance and keep changing the angle of the rearview mirror because you are slumping down in your seat from fatigue. The next time you get in the car, the mirror is too low. Slouching will absolutely kill you in chipping and putting, because the lower you bend at address, the more likely you will raise up in the forward swing.

You should realize when you analyze your results that just because you three-putted several times in a round doesn't mean you didn't putt well. It could have been caused by something that had nothing to do with your putting. For instance, in the Los Angeles Open one year, at Rancho Park, I three-putted four times. Afterwards, I went to the putting green and waited for my caddie, Walter Montgomery, to show up. I waited quite a while and finally spotted Walter at the practice range. Well, I got really upset with him and told him I wanted to practice putting. He said he knew that, but then he asked me if I realized that three out of the four three-putt greens that day came after I'd hit 5-irons on the green but well to the right of the pins and in difficult places to putt from. So I practiced with my 5-iron and discovered that the shaft was slightly bent. That was the main reason I was hitting that club to the right.

The message? Don't always overanalyze and overcorrect your putting. You have to find a balance, as in all things. But you must always be aware of what results you are getting for your efforts, be prepared to adjust, and be sure it is the putting itself that is the problem.

Chipping: It's Putting of a Different Kind

The reason I want to include a small section on chipping is because, in terms of technique alone, shots from just off the green are directly related to putting. I break chips down into two categories: Low Chip and High Chip.

Low Chips

Low chips don't have to clear anything but the fringe grass to reach the putting surface. This type makes up most of the chipping we do. You can use anything from a sand wedge to a 6-iron, depending on the distance you have to carry to get to the green and the undulation of the terrain you are chipping to. If the shot is downhill with only 20 feet of green from the edge of the fringe to the cup, a sand wedge or pitching wedge will get the ball onto the green with enough spin on the ball to keep it from running too quickly down the slope. For uphillers, of course, you should use a less-lofted club, if you have enough green to work with. There are a lot of choices here in terms of shot and club selection, and I don't think there is any one "system" that works. However, I do think there is a technique to recommend for playing these shots, one that is closely allied to putting.

Unlike when I putt, on low chips I play the ball very close to my toes—around 8 to 10 inches. Therefore, because I want my hands to be as vertical as when I putt, the club is set on its toe, the heel slightly off the ground. Most people stand the same distance from their ball for chipping as they do for full-swing shots. The result is that their hands are too low at address—the sole of the club is flush to the ground—and the heel of the club hits the ground first in the forward stroke. This can change the face angle at impact. It is even worse when playing out of longish grass. The heel can snag in it, twisting the face even more out of line with the target. And a nice smooth follow-through is almost impossible.

I almost always chip with the heel raised off the

ground. This means I don't often hit the ball on the sweetspot; usually I make contact close to the toe. But this doesn't produce a weak shot, as you might expect, nor does it cause the clubface to lose its angle at impact. That's because the swing is relatively soft, and so is the impact. We are talking about a little chip, after all.

Another difference between putts and low chips. For the latter, *do not choke down on the club* at address. However, you might want to use your putting grip for these chips. I sometimes do. In any case, hold the club full length so you can be sure of standing tall at the ball. You'll also see the line better and are less likely to rise up at impact. At least 65 percent of your weight should be on your left side. Aim the clubface square to the target but align your feet and body to the left of it. Most people think they're aiming directly at the line with their body when chipping, when in fact they are aligned to the right of it and the ball ends up going to the right. What's more, the right hand becomes too active in the takeaway and overpowers the stroke through impact. When you open your stance, your left hand does the work—and you can practice this by hitting chips with only your left hand.

Opening your stance also stops your body from moving. The angle of your right foot is especially important, because it prevents movement to the right as the swing begins.

The stroke is low going back and low going

For the low, running chip shot, stand tall for a good view of the target and close to the ball with your hands nearly vertical. Hold the club full length—don't choke up on it—and have the heel of the club off the ground. Address the ball a bit right of the club's sweetspot and make contact there.

For this low, running chip, play the ball back in
your stance, just inside the right heel. Weight is 65
percent on your left side (foot), and the stroke is
low back and low through, just as when putting.
There is no breakdown of the wrists, just a slight
hinging going back that is held to and through impact.

through, with only your hands and arms moving. You should feel as though you are pushing and pulling the club back and through, from low to low, with the left hand. Make sure you contact the ball first and keep the handle of the club and your hands as vertical at the finish of the stroke as they were at address—just as in putting. The butt of the club should not point back toward your body.

High Chips

These shots are hit from close to the green, high enough to clear the corner of a bunker, say, or some long grass.

The high chip is played much like a sand shot. The ball is positioned forward in your stance; how far forward depends on how much height you need. Your weight at address should be on your left side, but not quite as much as for low chips. For these shots you do not want to use your putting grip, because now you will want your right hand to be a little freer in the action.

Stand a bit farther back from the ball than for low chips, but still rest the club on its toe. Your hands will not be quite as vertical; in fact, the left wrist will have a bit of an inward cup. This is because when hitting this shot you want the left hand basically to stop right after impact. This is more of a "right-hand" shot, because you want higher trajectory and some backspin—or at least a soft landing.

For the high chip, the ball is played more forward in the stance—somewhere left of center, depending on how much height you need. You are a bit less vertical at address than for the low chip, and you stand a little farther back from the ball. Weight is not quite as left-side oriented. Again, the ball is set just right of the sweetspot.

There is more wrist hinge going back, and the right hand is more active in the forward stroke. It works under as if you are throwing a ball underhanded. Always use a sand wedge for this shot.

You'll get that by having your right hand move as though you're throwing a ball underhand.

Always use the sand wedge for high chips. And don't worry about snagging the heel in long grass or bouncing it off firm ground; setting the club on its toe at address solves that. And, again, don't be afraid to catch the ball slightly toward the toe of the clubface. Actually, that kind of contact helps deaden the ball and makes it land softly.

CHAPTER 5

Choosing Your Weapon

Light Is Right

No single golf club has more different designs than the putter. There probably are a thousand models on the market right now, and each is at least a little different. And no one knows how many thousands of other putter designs have had their day on the market and now are stashed in the dark corners of basements all over North America. The proliferation of designs says something about the creativity of those who come up with them but more about golfers themselves. They think, believe, or *want* to believe that it is the club—and *only* the club—that makes putts and that once they get the right weapon their troubles will be over. They also know, deep down, that such thinking is merely wishful. That said, I do not subscribe to the notion that a good putter can get the ball in the hole with anything—a broom, a ball-peen hammer, a shovel. It happens that the game's best putters have used clubs that have been fairly simple in design. But whatever its shape or overall length, a good putter is not too heavy, has a head (or face) that produces a soft feel, and, of course, is well balanced.

Weight may be the most important single component in putting with feel, and I'm convinced that a relatively light putter is best. Golfers who use heavy putters think this will guarantee they won't come up short. They really do believe the club is the solution, and as a result, the putter swings them instead of the other way around. But letting an inanimate object dictate your performance doesn't make a lot of sense. Heavy putters, which are mainly heavy in the head, make it difficult for the left hand to swing through with a controlled flow. Grip pressure will almost always be too tight, for one thing, and the right hand will become too dominant. In strictly mechanical terms, when the left hand is subservient to the right hand, it breaks down during the forward stroke, becoming cupped at impact. The blade comes up, and the ball is hit instead of rolled. The hit is heavy, and gauging the speed of the putt is difficult, or at best inconsistent.

I can't put a hard number on what a putter should

weigh. As you probably have gathered by now, I don't like to think in such terms. Instead, experiment a little with different putters and soon you will know what is heavy and what is not. And if you can't come to a decision, err on the side of a lighter one. Most good putters use lightweight putters. Ben Crenshaw with his Wilson 8802 and Bob Charles with his Acushnet Bullseye are good examples. The Ray Cook putter I used on the regular tour was about as light as those two.

Soft Goods

On the Senior Tour I have used an Odyssey putter quite a lot. It's about the same weight as my Ray Cook, but it has another feature that makes it especially effective, one that touches on another important aspect to selecting a putter—the material that a clubhead or clubface is made of. The Odyssey is distinctive for its thermoplastic insert (its trade name is "Stronomic"), which produces a soft feel at impact. I'm not suggesting that you use an Odyssey, but I do think you should get a putter that has a head made from a soft metal. Softer metals have become especially important now that just about every golfer uses a Surlyn-covered ball, which is quite hard compared to balata. Softer metal heads may reduce the speed at which a Surlyn-covered ball comes off the face of the putter, but perhaps more important, a soft metal head has a nicer feel than the traditional steel.

We're also seeing more putters with milled faces. Milling is meant to grind faces perfectly smooth, with no minuscule imperfections that might send a ball off line. Milling can increase the price of a putter significantly, and I'm not sure it is worth it in respect to the promised results, but I do know that the milling process can give you the precise loft you want. This way, you don't have to bend the hosel of the club to adjust the loft and risk altering the lie angle.

Loft on It

I don't understand how a golfer can even consider using a putter with no loft. The idea, I suppose, is to prevent the ball from jumping at impact and bouncing and skidding for a foot or so before rolling. Fine, but the disadvantages far outweigh that one and only advantage. It is easier to putt well when you start with your hands ahead of the ball, which is where the forward press puts them. When you use a putter with no loft, you are going to instinctively set your hands behind the ball at address. I've never seen anyone putt well, at least consistently well, from that position.

Shaft Flex

Not many golfers consider shaft flex when choosing a putter. Just about every putter off the rack has a stiff shaft—they are shafts for irons cut down to size —and they seem to work okay. With a stiff shaft you don't get any "snap" at the bottom of the stroke that might throw the ball off line—a good thing for average or poor putters. However, a shaft with a little more "give" will allow better feel. I wouldn't recommend a whippy shaft (like the old Spalding "Cash-In" putters had), but I've always liked a putter shaft that is a little thinner and lighter, or *softer.*

The Sweetspot

Most putterheads have some sort of marking on the top that is meant to indicate the sweetspot, the point on the putter face where you get the most solid hit. Hit the ball on either side of the sweetspot and the face will open or close and throw the ball off line. But I don't believe there is a single, small area of the club that gives you a solid hit. I think a lot of the putter face does this, especially on heel-and-toe (perimeter) weighted putters. The marks on the putterheads, then, are not very accurate in respect to what they are there for.

But putters do have sweetspots, even if their function is misunderstood, and in my experience, they usually are a little inside the marks, more toward the heels of the clubs. The best way to determine it for yourself is to hold the putter at the butt end with your fingers, letting it dangle loosely, and poke the center of the clubface with a finger. If the head goes straight back and the face doesn't waver to one side or the other you've poked the sweetspot. If the blade opens or closes, the poked point is not the sweetspot.

Flat Grip

We discussed earlier the value of holding the putter with the thumbs running straight down the middle of the shaft, a position best attained with a paddle-type putter grip that is flat in front. It can be done with a round grip, but you'll have to work on it all the time; it won't come naturally. Why give yourself something extra to think about when there is no particular advantage to a round grip?

As for the width of the grip, the way to determine the right size is to hold the club and see where the fingers come to when they are wrapped around the handle. There should be a slight gap between the tips of the fingers and the pads of the hands. If there is too much space, the grip is too thick. People with smallish hands would do well to use a pistol grip, which has a kind of thin, arched extension at the back of the butt end. It is designed to help keep the left hand from breaking down during the forward stroke.

It has become popular to use an extra-wide, padded putter grip, which is supposed to keep you from getting too "wristy." Some people also claim this grip cures the yips. Perhaps, but a grip that is even a touch too wide reduces feel. If you err in grip diameter, err on the thin side.

Grip Material

I'm not sure that leather provides any more feel than a quality rubber grip, but whatever material you use *put a new grip on your putter every six months* or so, depending on how much you play.

Few golfers think about the condition of their putter grip. Perhaps they feel that because the force of the stroke with a putter is so slight compared to full-swing shots, the grip is not important. They are wrong.

The sweat from your hands is more likely to get into the putter grip than the grips of your other clubs. You may handle a driver for a minute per shot, perhaps sixteen times a round. But you handle your putter far more often and for longer periods each time. It's not so much that the putter grip wears out, although that will happen eventually. It's that it gets hard and slippery, so much so that you have to squeeze it to get a firm hold, and that means tension and loss of feel.

Lie Angle—Get a Rocker Sole

Because the hands and club should be close to vertical during the stroke, the lie angle on your putter should be fairly flat. That is, when you set the blade down with the sole flush to the ground, the shaft should be fairly upright or vertical.

However, you will not always stand the same way at the ball. The terrain may force you to stand a bit farther from it; for example, if the ball is on a sidehill slope, where your feet are below the ball. If the slope runs away from you on the other hand, you must stand a little closer. Then there may be days when you just *feel* better standing a little farther or closer to the ball or more upright in your posture. You should go with that feeling.

However, because you can't change the lie angle of your putter for every round, or shot, and because the adjustment will never be drastic, your best bet is to use a putter with a "rocker" sole, one that is not perfectly flat. A rounded putter sole allows you to alter the angle just enough to suit your feel and still stroke the ball properly.

Putter Length

The length of your putter depends not on how tall you are, but on how long your arms are. The correct length allows you to keep your arms as straight as possible at address (with your left hand *completely* on the handle). This has led to a lot more golfers using shorter putters, 34 or 35 inches, which is what I use. It allows good arm extension, while maintaining proper posture. If you find yourself crouching too much over the ball with a shorter putter, go to one an inch or two longer.

Mallet or Blade: Sometimes a Change Is a Very Good Thing

I prefer a mallet-head putter, mainly because you can see its loft more easily than on a blade putter. I also like the appearance of "mass" behind the ball, which you don't get with blades. The look of a putter goes a long way in making you feel comfortable.

But let me say at this point that it is a good idea to change putters every so often. It should be a radical change, from a mallet to a blade or vice versa. You might also try a different type of shaft, or more or less loft, or more or less weight. The only thing that should remain the same is the lie angle. The main thing is that it looks different. I sometimes switch from a mallet to a blade putter, just because I dislike blades so much. With a thin blade at the bottom of the shaft, it doesn't look like there is enough club for me to get the ball to the hole, and that makes me stroke the ball more instead of letting the heavier seeming mallet-head do it for me.

But more important: When you go back to your regular putter it looks and feels much better. You're glad to have it back in your hands, and you immediately begin putting better. Your spirits are refreshed. In 1993, I won five tournaments on the Senior Tour, three with one putter, two with my "backup."

You also may change to suit different conditions. On slow greens, for example, you don't want to change your stroke; just use a slightly heavier putter or put some lead tape on your current putter.

To prepare for all possible circumstances, practice with different putters.

On the Care and Feeding of Your Putter

Whether you use a mallet or a blade, an aluminum or steel putter, it should not be shiny. The sun reflects off them, and you can't always see the face at address. The glare also will affect your eyesight when you look up from your putter to look at the line and the target. Why people use such putters is beyond me.

One last tip: Keep a headcover on your putter. This protects the face from bumps and dents that can affect the way the ball comes off the blade. This is especially important if your putter is made of soft metal. And if you're too lazy to use a headcover, at least store the putter with the longest clubs in your bag, up with the driver, spoon, and 5-wood and not with the short irons, where it will get banged up. I've seen some old Wilson 8802s and Acushnet Bullseyes that are worth a lot of money as relics but look like they've been beaten with a hammer.

Who knows, if you treat your putter well it may very well treat you the same way.

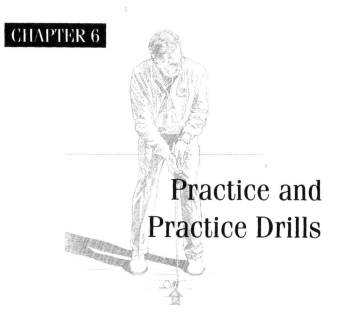

CHAPTER 6

Practice and
Practice Drills

As I mentioned in the foreword, my father understood something that scientific research would verify many years later, that it takes humans roughly three weeks to form or change a habit of mind or body. Therefore, if you decide to incorporate any of my suggestions on grip, stance, stroke, etc. be patient. It will take some twenty-one days before each idea transfers from a conscious effort to where you can perform it more or less subconsciously. The grip might take a little longer. It seems that changing one's grip is the hardest thing for people to do.

Then again, you can accelerate the process. You don't have to be on a golf course to practice a new grip or stance, and you can also practice a new stroke on a carpet at home or in your office. But it should be on a carpet similar to a putting green, for practicing on a thick, shag rug is not going to be very helpful.

Keep in mind, too, that new ideas must be adopted one at a time. I'm sure you have experienced the frustration of working on two different swing ideas at once and not doing either very well. It's just the way we are.

And you should not be thinking about mechanics on the golf course. Any changes you make to your technique should be worked out on the practice green.

Practice Sessions: Short in Duration, Long on Intensity

Because practicing your putting can be tough on your back, even if your back is in good shape, practice sessions should be fairly short. The great Henry Cotton, British Open champion in 1934, 1937, and 1948, came close to ending his career before it even got off the ground because he was so intent on improving his putting and spent hours bent over the ball on a practice green.

Odd though it may seem, putting is just as hard, if not harder, on your back as hitting full-swing shots. This may be because most golfers practice by hitting a number of putts without straightening up.

One solution is to use a longer-than-standard putter so you don't bend as much. Ray Floyd did this, although he has stopped short of using the superlong putters that have become so popular in the past few years. But if you practice with a longer putter, then that is the putter you must use when you play—just as you should always practice putting with the same type of ball you play with.

Of course, you could straighten up between practice putts. Which brings me to other aspects of practice that I believe are important. First, never practice with more than two balls. Most golfers use at least three balls to practice their putting, and some like to dump a whole shag bag out on the green and hit them one after the other and from the same angle. With all those balls out there, the tendency is to hit one after another in fairly rapid succession—hit and rake, hit and rake, as we say. You are apt to stay bent over, which is bad for your back, but you also become lax mentally. You lose focus on what you are trying to do and just keep bopping balls. Thoughtless strokes are poor strokes, and a lazy mind-set develops that is bound to leach into your on-course game.

Second, change the putt after each pair—two left-to-right breakers from 12 feet, a couple of right-to-left putts from 16 feet, and so on. You never have the same putt twice on the golf course, so you should simulate that in practice. The only time I putt from the same spot over and over again is when

I'm trying out a new putter. I know the speed and the break and don't have to consider that. I can just get the feel of the putter itself.

Another benefit of practice with two balls is that you will be inclined to take more time with each putt. We are talking maybe fifteen or twenty seconds between putts, a longer gap than it would seem. Stroke a putt, then count to twenty before you stroke the next one, and you'll see what I mean. It will seem an eternity compared to the time frame in which you probably practice. You can enhance this practice pace by letting the putterhead sit on the ground after each putt, which also will encourage the feeling of keeping the putter low through impact. Finally, after stroking a putt and letting the putterhead rest on the ground, watch the ball to the hole. If it goes in, congratulate yourself; enjoy the moment. If it misses, think about how it missed and consider why it didn't go in. (I also suggest you practice full-swing shots in the same way. As with putting, if you have more than two balls in front of you, you are especially susceptible to the hit-and-rake syndrome. After every shot I hit on the range, I hold my club up in the follow-through as I watch the flight of the ball, and as the ball begins to descend, I lower the club. I put it back on the ground only after the ball has landed.)

Preround Warmup

There are two kinds of putting practice—preround, and postround. Each serves a different purpose. But let me back up a little, to the driving range. Hitting a lot of full shots one after another will leave your hands a little numb, so always conclude this phase of your preround warmup by hitting soft pitch and chip shots. This will begin to restore the necessary feel to your fingers and hands.

In the preround putting warmup itself, you should not get involved in any mechanics, apart from hitting a few "spot putts," as I have described them. Spot putting is something you never get entirely used to, but because it is so effective you should do it as much as possible. As Ben Hogan once said, never try a shot on the golf course that you haven't practiced beforehand.

The main purpose of the preround warmup is to get a feel for the speed of the greens and for the conditions you will face on the course. If it's a windy day, for instance, stroke some putts with a little wider stance and with more weight on your left side, which helps prevent the wind from moving you. If you are to play greens with a lot of undulation, and the practice green is (as it *should* be) as undulated, practice a number of putts over and along sides of hills. (Augusta National springs to mind here as its practice green is identical in contours and speed to the greens on the course.) If the course has fairly flat, small greens, such as those at Pebble Beach or Harbour Town, I practice mostly shorter putts—from 12 feet or closer.

End every session by making a few two- and three-footers. This will get you off to the first tee with a good mind-set; you have just made a couple of putts and have had the experience of hearing the ball rattle in the cup and of taking it out of the hole.

In all, the preround putting warmup should last no longer than ten minutes. And of course, use only two balls.

Postround Putting Practice and Drills

Some people believe you can practice technique when playing a casual round by yourself or during a noncompetitive round with friends. I disagree. I am convinced that when you are playing golf, even during so-called casual rounds, you should work on *playing* the game—the mental process required to make a score. This is no time to think about mechanics, and what you do under "casual" circumstances will feed into your play when the game is really on. Always shoot for a score, playing the shots as they arise. That is the best kind of on-course practice.

The time to work on technique is just *after* a round or when you have half an hour or so on a day when you don't plan to play. Postround practice can be especially valuable, because how you have just putted is fresh in your mind. The lesson here is fairly obvious. Work on the type of putts you missed on the course. As I mentioned in chapter 4, if you missed a few right-to-left putts to the left your hands may be a bit too low at address. Practice getting them more vertical. If you missed these putts to the right—hit them too high—you may have forward pressed too much or your hands may have been too vertical; although it's best to putt with your hands relatively vertical, they sometimes can get too "high."

If you didn't get left-to-right breaking putts high enough, stroke some practice putts with more weight on your left side and your hands a little lower at address. If you are hitting the ball too far past the hole, work on a softer stroke.

Postround practice putting should last no more than twenty to thirty minutes. You've been out on the course for three to four hours, often longer, and probably will have a difficult time keeping your energy level high enough to make the practice session worthwhile. And when your concentration ebbs, the practice can hurt your game. Sometimes, ten minutes can be enough. If you've found some answers to the problems you had on the course, be satisfied and stop.

And never dwell on your putting away from the course. That's pretty hard to do, I'll grant you; everyone who is serious about golf tends to think about it a lot, if not all the time. But try, once off the course, to let it be. Especially if you have found a good feel in your postround practice.

Putting Drills

There are no specific drills for learning to stand slightly bowlegged at address, for gripping the putter with both thumbs down the center of the handle, for having your weight distributed in a certain way, and other more or less static elements of putting technique. You just think about and do these things when you practice. However, there are some drills I can recommend that will help develop a sounder stroke, a feel for speed and distance, and an ability to find the right line and stroke the ball along it.

Chalk-Line Drill

One effective drill involves making a carpenter chalk line on the practice green, from six to eight feet long. You hold a chalked string taut at the ends and flick it. Some course superintendents may not like it, but the chalk doesn't do the grass any harm. The idea is to stroke along the line, starting from the middle and working your way back to one end.

This drill is valuable for several reasons. One, it

teaches you to set your head correctly. Most golfers unwittingly look to the right of the line at address. It may have to do with the angle of the putter and the golfer's position beside the ball. Whatever the reason, there is a tilt of the head to the right, as though you are looking around a corner, and the view is not true to the desired line. The chalk line gives you a guide to set your head and eyes directly and squarely over the ball, and running your eyes along the chalk line gets you into the habit of looking down the true line.

The chalk line also helps you check that the blade of your putter is square to your line. But this only applies if a parallel line runs across the top of your putter head. You match up the chalk line and this line. A dot mark on the top of the putter won't help much.

I believe that if I set my hands on the club square, with my thumbs straight up and down on the front of the grip, the blade *has* to be square. You can hand me a putter in a dark closet and, if the grip has a flat front and I put my hands on it correctly, I assure you that the face will be square when I put it down on the floor.

Using Tees to Train Your Eye and Touch

One of the first drills I learned from my father was to put a tee in the ground 16 inches behind the hole and make a point of never hitting the ball past it. In a way, the tee serves the same purpose as the tree in the middle of the fairway we talked about earlier; it provides an actual visual entity that helps you focus on how you want to shape the trajectory of the ball.

This drill should be used for all types of putts—downhillers, uphillers, sidehillers, and flat ones. You want to be prepared for everything you may face on the golf course, which, along with altering or sharpening your mechanics, is the point of practice.

Another drill is, on a putt with no break put a tee in the ground about a quarter-inch from the hole, right in front of it. Then try to make six-footers with the ball going in on each side of the tee. A hole is about three balls wide, so there's room on each side. This drill is fun to do, which is as it should be. Practice doesn't have to be hard labor. And of course, the value of the drill is to develop a smooth and precise stroke. You can't go hammering at the ball when you're trying to get it around that tee.

This drill also helps you learn to putt at the corners of the hole, which is what you do on all breaking putts, but especially the shorter ones.

Here's one more drill using a tee—one that is particularly valuable in helping you understand and sense where the center of the hole really is in relation to your line. As I said earlier, most putts are breaking putts, and the target you should be aiming for is that point at the cup where you expect the

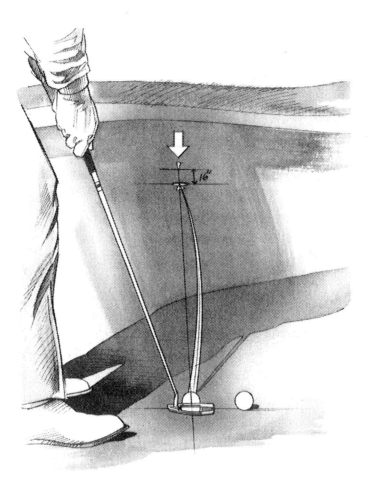

*An excellent practice drill for learning to feel speed
and distance is to place a tee in the green 16 inches
directly behind the hole and make a point of never
hitting the ball past that tee.*

To develop a smooth, roll-the-ball stroke, place a tee in the ground about a quarter inch directly in front of the hole for a dead-straight putt and try to get the ball in the hole from either side of the tee.

Practicing with a tee in front of the hole might seem difficult at first, but after several strokes you'll find yourself holing more putts than not. This drill is also valuable in learning to putt for the corners of the hole.

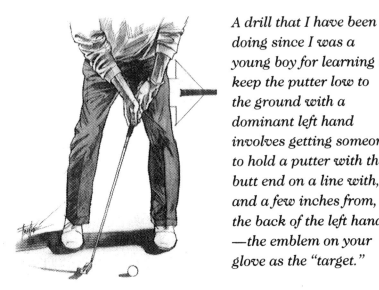

A drill that I have been doing since I was a young boy for learning to keep the putter low to the ground with a dominant left hand involves getting someone to hold a putter with the butt end on a line with, and a few inches from, the back of the left hand —the emblem on your glove as the "target."

In stroking the ball, your goal is to hit the butt of that club with the emblem on your glove.

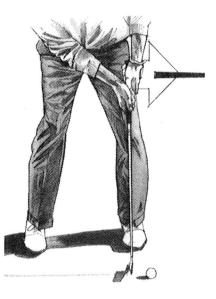

If you hit it with the center of the emblem, your stroke was just right. (If you hit it above the emblem, you have been even better. If you hit it below the emblem, you have made a poor stroke and lifted the putter up.)

ball to enter. So, put a tee in the ground at the very edge of the cup at that point where you expect the ball to enter, then try to hit it with your putt. The tee once again provides a tangible visual obstacle that helps you focus on your task.

Keep the Blade Low

Because I think it is so important that the putterhead be kept as low as possible during the entire stroke, a drill I often use is to stroke the ball then put the clubhead on the ground after finishing the stroke. Just set it down there, *with the club in your hands still in a vertical position.* Most golfers will have the butt of the club angling backward at their waist at the finish of their stroke, an indication that they have come up instead of keeping the blade low through impact and follow-through.

A Drill for Left-Hand Dominance

I mentioned this drill earlier, in brief, but want to elaborate here, because this is an excellent drill for getting the feel for the left hand being dominant in the stroke. Stroke only with your left hand on the club. You don't even have to hit balls. To keep control of the club, choke down on the grip with your left hand, even a little on the shaft if necessary. Keep the rest of the handle up against your forearm when you stroke. If the handle comes off the forearm, it is because you raised the putter up, or flipped it.

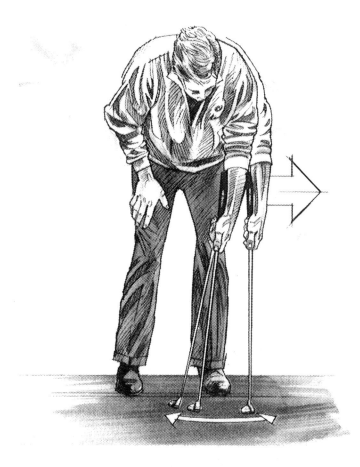

One way to develop a good sense of left-hand dominance in the stroke: Hold the putter with only your left hand and stroke the ball. Choke well down on the handle and rest the remainder of the handle against your forearm. Keep the handle against your forearm when stroking the ball. If the handle comes off, you know you have made a flip stroke.

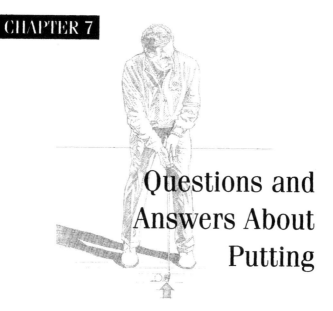

CHAPTER 7

Questions and Answers About Putting

Over the years many golfers have asked me about putting. What follows are some of the most frequent and interesting queries. (This also is a good opportunity to deal with aspects of putting that somehow don't fit into the narrative flow of an instruction book.)

Q: Jack Nicklaus has described his putting stroke as a kind of pushing of the club into the ball. Other top putters have said they feel they are pulling the club to impact with their left hand. Do you push or pull?
STOCKTON: Neither. I *roll* the ball.

Q: When do you putt from off the green?

STOCKTON: Only on a well-manicured course, such as Augusta National, where you can putt from as far as 10 yards off the green and there is little resistance to the roll of the ball. Also, there mustn't be too much difference between the length and speed of the grass on the fairway and fringe and the grass on the green.

Q: Should you ever putt out of a bunker?

STOCKTON: If there is no lip and the sand is hard, it can make sense to putt—if you have very little green to work with and it is tough to stop the ball with a wedge shot. I putted out of greenside bunkers twice when I won my first pro tournament, the 1967 Colonial Invitational. In both cases the pins were extremely close to where my ball was in the bunker. All I needed was to get the ball out of the trap and I would be pretty close. I got up and down both times.

Q: Do you do anything different when putting with a Surlyn-covered ball, compared to one with a balata cover?

STOCKTON: I don't make a different stroke, just hit the ball more softly. Surlyn balls come off the putter face faster, which means they don't break as much. I prefer balata because I get better feel on chips and putts.

Q: Is any special physical conditioning necessary for putting?

STOCKTON: Putting is not about strength, so it doesn't require flexibility exercises or weight lifting. It is a matter of hand-eye coordination, and you should do anything you can to help develop and refine it. I feel putts better if I shoot pool the night before. I also do needlepoint, occasionally, which also helps. Fly-fishing would be another good exercise.

Q: What is the best way to approach a breaking putt?
STOCKTON: Concentrate on the speed of a putt and always err on the high side. A putt hit to the high side always has a chance of going in, if the speed is close to right. A putt not hit high enough, no matter its speed, has no chance. If you must err, overread to the high side, but roll the ball softly. You put the odds in your favor.

Q: Do you always play short putts inside the hole?
STOCKTON: Yes, I play almost every short putt inside the hole, but I very seldom play a putt straight into the hole.

Q: Which part of the ball itself do you envision going in on short putts?
STOCKTON: I envision the whole ball, not just part of it, going over the edge of the hole. The cups on tour are painted white for television, and sometimes a ball that has been rammed into the hole will knock some of the paint off. That chipped spot can give me a good target. One reason I'm a pretty good putter is

that I have so many different images of the ball going in. Most golfers have an image of how they are going to *make* it go in with a mechanical effort. But reading the line and *seeing* the ball go in is where good putting starts.

Q: How do you find the best ball position in your stance?

STOCKTON: The ball should always be somewhere between the inside of your left heel and the center of your stance, but you should not be locked into one position. It will vary according to the undulation of the terrain or the speed of the green. On a fast green you should position the ball a little farther back, because you want to take a relatively short backstroke. On slower greens it should be farther forward, because you will be making a longer stroke.

Q: On breaking putts, do you aim for the apex of the break, the point where you expect the ball to begin changing direction? Is it a straight putt to that point?

STOCKTON: None of the above. While in the initial read of a putt I will break it down into thirds as I've described earlier, when it comes to stroking the ball the total curvature of the putt all the way to the hole, is the only thing in your mind.

Q: On certain kinds of putts, say fast downhillers or sharp breaking ones, do you ever set the ball on the outside or inside of the putter face?

STOCKTON: For the most part I align the ball with the same spot on the putter face, although on extremely fast downhill putts I will put the ball slightly toward the toe. Still, if you have a soft touch and use a light putter, you shouldn't have to do that.

Q: You seem to imitate Nicklaus in your style of putting. Was he an influence?
STOCKTON: Actually, I think I'm the total opposite of Jack. That's one reason why I hesitate to consider him a great putter, even though he has won more majors than anyone else. Fundamentally, he does three things I think are wrong: 1. His grip is out of balance—the left hand neutral, on top of the handle, the right hand way under. 2. He dips his right shoulder down so that he is looking more or less down the line from behind the ball. 3. He stands over the ball too long. Too long, that is, for anyone but Jack.

The lesson to be learned from Jack, however, is that any method will work if you can do it consistently. That means working on it—concentrating on your putting as much, if not more, than every other part of your game. I can tell you that for all the splendid shots Jack has hit from tee to green, if he wasn't as good as he was with the putter he wouldn't have won nearly as much.

Q: What is one myth about putting?
STOCKTON: "Never up, never in." I'll grant you, if you're short on a putt it's never going in, but if you

are only one inch short it's unlikely you'll three-putt. And if you eliminate three or four three-putt greens per round, all of a sudden your handicap goes down and you haven't even sunk any long putts. Constantly going well past the hole is far worse than coming up a few inches short every now and then.

Q: What do people ask you most about putting?
STOCKTON: Most of the questions have to do with the stroke, but what I *should* be asked is how to develop feel for putting and picturing the ball going in. People who want to know about the mechanical nature of putting are getting the cart before the horse. Putting is primarily about feel and visualization.

Afterword

You now have everything I know about putting—all the mechanics, all the technique. The amount of material and how it has been presented is in synch with what I believe is at the heart of good putting: *feel*. Therefore, I have not cluttered things up with putting statistics or a lot of technical language. I have tried to project the idea that good putting is a matter of having a sound, positive image of every putt before you hit it. But I want to stress again that the picture is not the kind in which you connect numbered dots. That is a mechanistic approach that detracts from the kind of free-spirited sense of lightness that makes putting fun and also more rewarding. If I have stimulated you to look forward to putting, to be intrigued by it, then I have done what I set out to do. That you will also make better scores because of that attitude is really only a bonus.

—D. S.

About the Authors

DAVE STOCKTON has long been recognized as one of the outstanding putters in the history of the game. His eleven PGA Tour victories—including two major championships, the 1970 and 1976 PGA Championships—and his eleven victories to date on the Senior Tour are testaments to his skill. When not touring, he lives in Mentone, California.

AL BARKOW has been writing professionally about golf for over 30 years. He has published nine books on golf, including several histories of the PGA Tour and instructionals written with Billy Casper, Ken Venturi, Phil Rodgers, Carl Lohren, and George Low. He is currently editor-in-chief of *Golf Illustrated* magazine. He lives in Montclair, New Jersey.

Made in the USA